GRADES **6-8**

MATH

Activities for the
Differentiated
Classroom

Gayle H. Gregory • Carolyn Chapman

CORWIN PRESS
Classroom

For information:

Corwin Press
A SAGE Publications Company
2455 Teller Road
Thousand Oaks, California 91320
CorwinPress.com

SAGE Publications, Ltd.
1 Oliver's Yard
55 City Road
London EC1Y 1SP
United Kingdom

SAGE Publications India Pvt. Ltd.
B 1/I 1 Mohan Cooperative
Industrial Area
Mathura Road, New Delhi
India 110 044

SAGE Publications Asia-Pacific Pvt. Ltd.
33 Pekin Street #02-01
Far East Square
Singapore 048763

Printed in the United States of America.

ISBN 978-1-4129-5342-9

This book is printed on acid-free paper.

08 09 10 11 12 10 9 8 7 6 5 4 3 2 1

Executive Editor: Kathleen Hex
Managing Developmental Editor: Christine Hood
Editorial Assistant: Anne O'Dell
Developmental Writer: Susan Ludwig
Developmental Editor: Karen Hall
Proofreader: Bette Darwin
Art Director: Anthony D. Paular
Cover Designer: Monique Hahn
Interior Production Artists: Lisa Riley and Karine Hovsepian

GRADES **6–8**

| MATH |

Activities for the
Differentiated
Classroom

TABLE OF CONTENTS

Connections to Standards **4**

Introduction **6**

Put It Into Practice **7**

CHAPTER 1
Numbers and Operations **9**
Activities and reproducibles

CHAPTER 2
Algebra **28**
Activities and reproducibles

CHAPTER 3
Geometry **44**
Activities and reproducibles

CHAPTER 4
Measurement **71**
Activities and reproducibles

CHAPTER 5
Data Analysis and Probability **84**
Activities and reproducibles

Answer Key **95**

References **96**

Connections to Standards

This chart shows the national mathematics standards that are covered in each chapter.

NUMBERS AND OPERATIONS	Standards are covered on pages
Understand numbers, ways of representing numbers, relationships among numbers, and number systems.	9, 23
Understand meanings of operations and how they relate to one another.	11, 13, 14
Compute fluently, and make reasonable estimates.	13, 14, 17, 23, 26

ALGEBRA	Standards are covered on pages
Understand patterns, relations, and functions.	37, 38, 40, 42
Represent and analyze mathematical situations and structures using algebraic symbols.	28, 30, 32, 40, 42
Use mathematical models to represent and understand quantitative relationships.	40, 42
Analyze change in various contexts.	40

GEOMETRY	Standards are covered on pages
Analyze characteristics and properties of two- and three-dimensional geometric shapes, and develop mathematical arguments about geometric relationships.	44, 51, 56, 57, 62, 67
Specify locations and describe spatial relationships using coordinate geometry and other representational systems.	49

MEASUREMENT	Standards are covered on pages
Understand measurable attributes of objects and the units, systems, and processes of measurement.	67, 73, 80, 83
Apply appropriate techniques, tools, and formulas to determine measurements.	67, 71, 73, 80

DATA ANALYSIS AND PROBABILITY	Standards are covered on pages
Select and use appropriate statistical methods to analyze data.	84, 86, 88
Develop and evaluate inferences and predictions based on data.	84, 86
Understand and apply basic concepts of probability.	89, 92

PROBLEM SOLVING	Standards are covered on pages
Solve problems that arise in mathematics and in other contexts.	17

Introduction

As a teacher who has adopted the differentiated philosophy, you design instruction to embrace the diversity of the unique students in your classroom and strategically select tools to build a classroom where all students can succeed. This requires careful planning and a very large toolkit! You must make decisions about what strategies and activities best meet the needs of the students in your classroom at that time. It is not a "one size fits all" approach.

When planning for differentiated instruction, include the steps described below. Refer to the planning model in *Differentiated Instructional Strategies: One Size Doesn't Fit All, Second Edition* (Gregory & Chapman, 2007) for more detailed information.

1. Establish standards, essential questions, and expectations for the lesson or unit.

2. Identify content, including facts, vocabulary, and essential skills.

3. Activate prior knowledge. Pre-assess students' levels of readiness for the learning and collect data on students' interests and attitudes about the topic.

4. Determine what students need to learn and how they will learn it. Plan various activities that complement the learning styles and readiness levels of all students in this particular class. Locate appropriate resources or materials for all levels of readiness.

5. Apply the strategies and adjust to meet students' varied needs.

6. Decide how you will assess students' knowledge. Consider providing choices for students to demonstrate what they know.

Differentiation does not mean always tiering every lesson for three levels of complexity or challenge. It does mean finding interesting, engaging, and appropriate ways to help students learn new concepts and skills. The practical activities in this book are designed to support your differentiated lesson plans. They are not pre-packaged units, but rather activities you can incorporate into your plan for meeting the unique needs of the students in your classroom right now. Use these activities as they fit into differentiated lessons or units you are planning. They might be used for total group lessons, to reinforce learning with individuals or small groups, to focus attention, to provide additional rehearsal opportunities, or to assess knowledge. Your differentiated toolkit should be brimming with engaging learning opportunities. Take out those tools and start building success for all your students!

Put It into Practice

Differentiation is a Philosophy

For years teachers planned "the lesson" and taught it to all students, knowing that some will get it and some will not. Faced with NCLB and armed with brain research, we now know that this method of lesson planning will not reach the needs of all students. Every student learns differently. In order to leave no child behind, we must teach differently.

Differentiation is a philosophy that enables teachers to plan strategically in order to reach the needs of the diverse learners in the classroom and to help them meet the standards. Supporters of differentiation as a philosophy believe:

- All students have areas of strength.

- All students have areas that need to be strengthened.

- Each student's brain is as unique as a fingerprint.

- It is never too late to learn.

- When beginning a new topic, students bring their prior knowledge base and experience to the new learning.

- Emotions, feelings, and attitudes affect learning.

- All students can learn.

- Students learn in different ways at different times.

The Differentiated Classroom

A differentiated classroom is one in which the teacher responds to the unique needs of the students in that room, at that time. Differentiated instruction provides a variety of options to successfully reach targeted standards. It meets learners where they are and offers challenging, appropriate options for them to achieve success.

Differentiating Content By differentiating content the standards are met while the needs of the particular students being taught are considered. The teacher strategically selects the information to teach and the best resources with which to teach it using different genres, leveling materials, using a variety of instructional materials, and providing choice.

Differentiating Assessment Tools Most teachers already differentiate assessment during and after the learning. However, it is equally important to assess what knowledge or interests students bring to the learning formally or informally.

Assessing student knowledge prior to the learning experience helps the teacher find out:

- What standards, objectives, concepts, skills the students already understand

- What further instruction and opportunities for mastery are needed

- What areas of interests and feelings will influence the topic under study

- How to establish flexible groups—total, alone, partner, small group

Differentiating Performance Tasks In a differentiated classroom, the teacher provides various opportunities and choices for the students to show what they've learned. Students use their strengths to show what they know through a reflection activity, a portfolio, or an authentic task.

Differentiating Instructional Strategies When teachers vary instructional strategies and activities, more students learn content and meet standards. By targeting diverse intelligences and learning styles, teachers can develop learning activities that help students work in their areas of strength as well as areas that still need strengthening.

Some of these instructional strategies include:

- Graphic organizers

- Cubing

- Role-playing

- Centers

- Choice boards

- Adjustable assignments

- Projects

- Academic contracts

When planning, teachers in the differentiated classroom focus on the standards, but also adjust and redesign the learning activities, tailoring them to the needs of the unique learners in each classroom. Teachers also consider how the brain operates and strive to use research-based, best practices to maximize student learning. Through differentiation we give students the opportunity to learn to their full potential. A differentiated classroom engages students and facilitates learning so all learners can succeed!

CHAPTER 1

Numbers and Operations

Guess What I Am

Standard
Numbers and Operations—Understand numbers, ways of representing numbers, relationships among numbers, and number systems.

Objective
Students will use their knowledge of place value to write number riddles.

A firm foundation in place value is essential for understanding higher-level math concepts and the power of methods and operations. Having students practice place value by writing riddles appeals to verbal/linguistic learners and develops students' critical thinking skills

1. Ahead of time, write this riddle on the board or on chart paper:

   I am a six-digit number
   As odd as can be.
   Divide me by 3,
   And you'll get 152,263.
   If you add up my digits
   All in a line,
   You'll end up with
   The odd number 39.
   In case you are not sure
   If you know me yet,
   My first digit is smaller
   Than all the rest.
   What number am I? (456,789)

2. Read the riddle aloud, and solve it together, highlighting the clues.

3. Brainstorm other clues a place-value riddle could contain (e.g., information about whether the number or any digits are prime or composite, odd or even, perfect squares, or palindromes). Write this information on the board for students to refer to as they write their own riddles.

4. After pre-assessing students' place-value readiness, divide the class into like-ability groups of two or three. Encourage groups

to write a riddle according to their ability. For example, have beginning mastery students write about numbers in the hundred thousands; approaching mastery students, numbers in the billions; high mastery students, decimals, exponents, or square roots.

5. As students work on their riddles, walk around the room, encouraging and assisting groups as needed.

6. Team groups together to exchange and solve each other's riddles.

Ideas for More Differentiation

Use students' riddles for a sponge activity. Have students write their riddles on one side of an index card and the answer on the other side. Keep the cards in a file box. Whenever you have a few extra minutes, pull a card from the file and read it aloud, letting students guess the number. Encourage students to add to the file throughout the year.

Extend the Activity

Have students write prime and composite number riddles. For example: *I am a composite number between 120 and 130. The sum of my digits is one less than the product of my digits.* (124)

Mighty Mnemonics

Standard
Numbers and Operations—Understand meanings of operations and how they relate to one other.

Objective
Students will use mnemonic devices to remember the order of operations.

A basic component for solving algebraic expressions and algebraic equations is following the correct order of operations. Students must work in an organized manner to arrive at the correct answer. However, remembering the steps can be difficult. Mnemonics is a rehearsal strategy that helps students remember the order of operations and engage their verbal/linguistic intelligences.

1. Write an equation on the board, such as: $20 \div (12 - 2) \times 3^2 + 2$. Explain the importance of solving the problem in the correct order, and discuss the order of operations:
   - **P**arentheses
   - **E**xponents
   - **M**ultiplication and **D**ivision (left to right)
   - **A**ddition and **S**ubtraction (left to right)

2. Use the Think-Pair-Share strategy to develop mnemonics. First, have each student think individually about words and phrases that could represent the first letter of each word in the order of operations (e.g., PEMDAS—**P**ink **E**lephants **M**ust **D**ance **A**nd **S**ing).

Pink Elephants Must Dance And Sing

3. Then have students work with partners to develop a mnemonic to share with the class. Invite them to illustrate their mnemonic, as well, to provide a memorable picture of their idea.

4. Invite the class to vote on which mnemonic is easiest to remember, which is funniest, which is cleverest, and so on.

Ideas for More Differentiation

- To engage students' musical intelligences, have students write a rhyme, rap, or song. Group the students according to their writing interests. Encourage them to make their work original but efficient so that it is memorable and useful.

- Let students who have a high degree of mastery with the order of operations create problems showing what occurs when operations are performed in the incorrect order.

Extend the Activity

Tap into your students' visual/spatial intelligences by having them make bookmarks of their order-of-operations mnemonic. For easy access, students can keep the bookmarks in their math books.

Fun with Fours

Standards
Numbers and Operations—Understand meanings of operations and how they relate to one another.
Compute fluently, and make reasonable estimates.

Strategies
Cooperative group learning

Journaling

Objective
Students will experiment with the order of operations to find a given number.

This mind-bending, cooperative learning activity focuses on understanding the meanings and effects of arithmetic operations and the order of operations. It also develops critical thinking and mathematical reasoning skills.

1. After pre-assessing students' basic computation ability, divide them into mixed-ability groups of three or four. Give each group a sheet of paper, and have them number their papers from *1* to *20*.

2. Write the number *4* on the chalkboard. The challenge is to write expressions that equal *1* to *20*, using only the number *4* and any combination of math operations, parentheses, and exponents. Demonstrate and discuss some examples on the board. For example: *To equal 2, the expression could be (4 + 4) ÷ 4; to equal 4, the expression could be (4 − 4) + 4.*

3. Review the order of operations: (1) Perform the operations inside parentheses. (2) Simplify exponents. (3) Multiply and divide left to right. (4) Add and subtract left to right.

4. Encourage groups to continue writing their own expressions for the remaining numbers. Then invite groups to share their expressions with the class and explain their strategies and methods for writing the expressions. List the various expressions on the board or on chart paper, and discuss.

5. Invite students to write in their journals, reflecting on their participation and learning. Prompt them with questions such as: *What did you notice about your participation in group learning? What did you notice about how your group worked together? Explain how the use of parentheses can affect an equation.*

Math Wheels

Standards

Numbers and Operations—Understand meanings of operations and how they relate to one another.

Compute fluently, and make reasonable estimates.

Objective

Students will experiment with numbers and order of operations to find expressions that equal a given number.

Materials

Math Wheels reproducible

Properly following the order of operations is a critical step in solving expressions and algebraic equations. Often, students are proficient in basic math skills but make errors when it comes to following the order of operations. This focus activity can be used to open students' "mental files" on basic computation skills and order of operations.

1. Review the order of operations with students: (1) Perform the operations inside parentheses. (2) Simplify exponents. (3) Multiply and divide left to right. (4) Add and subtract left to right.

2. Explain that there are many expressions that result in the same number value. Write *14* on the chalkboard. Explain that one way to express *14* using three operations and parentheses is *(18 ÷ 3) x 4 – 10*. Invite volunteers to offer several more expressionsusing three operations and resulting in 14. For example: *14 x 3 – (9 + 19)* and *(8 x 10) – 10 ÷ 5*.

3. Give students a copy of the **Math Wheels reproducible (page 16)**. Have them write a number in the center circle of each wheel (e.g., *14* and *116*). Then, in each section, write a math expression that has the same value as the number in the center circle. Have students use a minimum of three operations in each expression. Encourage students to use parenthesie, exponents, and the correct order of operations.

4. Invite students to share their expressions and methods for forming the expressions. Discuss the various solutions.

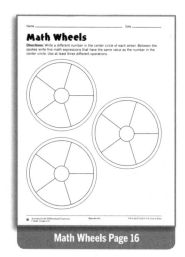

Math Wheels Page 16

Ideas for More Differentiation

- Challenge your high-degree mastery students to use four or more operations and larger numbers. Have beginning mastery students use two operations or two-step expressions using one operation. Provide calculators and manipulatives for students to use if they need help.

- Use the Think-Pair-Share strategy to come up with expressions. Write a number on the chalkboard, and have students think individually about a possible expression. Then have them work with partners to develop an expression to present to the class.

- Invite students to access their musical and linguistic abilities to write a poem or a rap of the expression. Encourage students to use mathematical terms such as *product*, *quotient*, *sum*, *difference*, and *equals*.

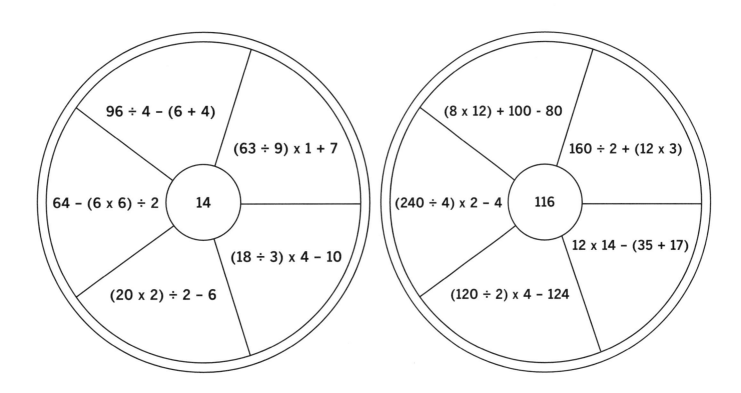

Math Wheels

Directions: Write a different number in the center circle of each wheel. Between the spokes, write five math expressions that have the same value as the number in the center circle. Use at least three different operations.

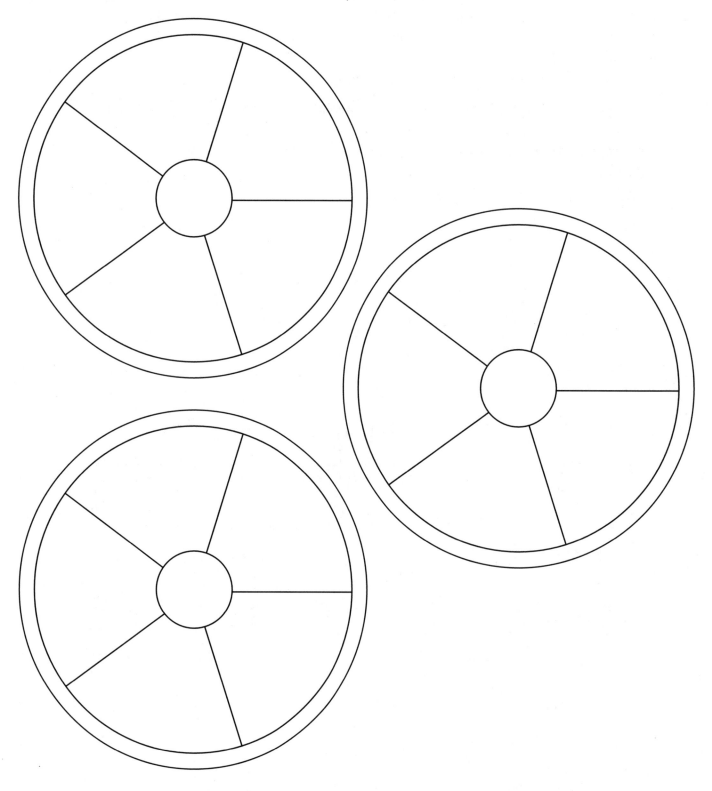

978-1-4129-5342-9 • © Corwin Press

Travel Plans

Standards
Numbers and Operations—Compute fluently, and make reasonable estimates.
Problem Solving—Solve problems that arise in mathematics and in other contexts.

Objective
Students will estimate and perform math operations by planning a trip within a designated budget.

Materials
Traveling the States reproducible
Airfare Expert reproducible
Hotel Expert reproducible
Rental Car Expert reproducible
newspaper travel section
travel magazines

Strategies
Authentic task

Cooperative group learning

Journaling

Make math come alive as students exercise their computational and social skills! This cooperative travel planning activity provides students with real-world skills they will use in their daily lives. Make sure to set aside multiple sessions for students to complete the activity.

1. Ask students: *If you could go on a trip anywhere in the United States, where would you go, and why?* Let students share their dream vacations. Then group students according to their interests and where they would like to visit.

2. Tell students that they will be working as a team to plan a six-day, five-night, three-person trip to a major U.S. city. Their budget is $4,500. Give students travel dates, such as *June 1–6*.

3. Distribute a copy of the **Traveling the States reproducible (page 19)** to each group, and discuss the task, roles, and process.

Travel Plans Page 19

Airfare Expert Page 20

4. Once group members have decided which roles they will assume, distribute the **Airfare Expert**, **Hotel Expert**, and **Rental Car Expert** **reproducibles (pages 20–22)** to each respective student. Allow time for students to complete their pages using the Internet, newspaper travel sections, and travel magazines.

5. Invite group members to meet and present their findings. Discuss whether their estimates were reasonable. As a group, make a final decision on each expense, and complete the travel plan itinerary.

6. Have each group present their travel plans to the class and share their rationale for choosing certain options.

7. Ask students to reflect on their participation and learning by writing in their journals. Prompt them with questions such as:
   - *In your role, why did you make certain choices?*
   - *In your role, what is one thing that you might have done differently?*
   - *Were your estimates reasonable?*
   - *Is there anything in your travel plans you would like to change? What is it?*
   - *Could your team have spent less money on this trip? If so, how?*
   - *Would you need more money for any other portion of this trip? If so, what?*

Ideas for More Differentiation

- As a class, decide on a city to visit. Have students form base groups of three in which they can "jigsaw" the research. Each member of the base group is assigned one of the expenses to research (airfare, hotel, car rental). All students with the same expense come together to research costs and options and then go back to their base groups to report their findings. The base groups use this information to complete the travel itinerary.

- Create a Travel Planning Center in which students can work individually or in pairs to develop an itinerary. Place newspapers, magazines (see Materials list), and a computer in the center. Have plenty of Traveling the States reproducibles available to help students record and organize their information.

Name _____ Date _____

Traveling the States

Directions: Follow these steps to plan a six-day, five-night, three-person trip to a major U.S. city. Your budget is $4,500. Your travel dates are _____.

1. As a group, decide which of these roles each group member will assume.

Airfare Expert _____

Hotel Expert _____

Rental Car Expert _____

2. Estimate how much to spend on airfare, hotel, and rental car.

3. Research your area of expertise. You may use newspapers, travel magazines, and the Internet.

4. Meet with your group and present your findings. Discuss whether your estimates are reasonable. As a group, make a final decision on each expense and complete the travel itinerary.

5. Present your travel itinerary to the class. Each member will explain various costs within his or her area and the team's rationale for choosing these options.

_____

Travel Itinerary from _____ to _____

Grand Total _____

Airline/Flight Number	Outbound Flight	Return Flight	Class	Taxes/Fees	Total Cost
	Depart	Depart			
	Arrive	Arrive			

Hotel Name	Location	Type of Room	Cost Per Night	Cost for 5 Nights	Taxes/Fees	Total Cost

Car Rental Company	Location	Car Type	Daily Rate	Cost for 5 Days	Taxes/Fees	Total Cost

Airfare Expert

Directions: Your job is to research costs for air travel. Consider various airlines, airports, times of travel, and classes of tickets. Compare prices. Search the Internet using the key word *airlines*. Use this chart to organize your research.

Name of Web Site, Newspaper, Magazine	Airline/ Flight	Depart	Arrive	Class	Taxes/ Fees	Total Cost

978-1-4129-5342-9 • © Corwin Press

Rental Car Expert

Directions: Your job is to research costs for rental cars. Consider various rental companies, car types, and rates. Compare prices. Search the Internet using the key words *rental cars*. Use this chart to organize your research.

Name of Web Site, Newspaper, Magazine	Leasing Company	Location	Car Type	Daily Rate	Cost for 5 days	Taxes/ Fees	Total Cost

Name _____ Date _____

Hotel Expert

Directions: Your job is to research costs for hotels. Consider hotel location, types of rooms, and amenities (pool, complimentary breakfast, gym). Compare prices. Search the Internet using the key words *hotel* and the city name. Use this chart to organize your research.

Name of Web Site, Newspaper, Magazine	Hotel Name and Address	Type of Room	Amenities	Cost Per Night	Cost for 5 Nights	Taxes/ Fees	Total Cost

Tasty Fractions and Percents

Standards

Numbers and Operations—Understand numbers, ways of representing numbers, relationships among number,s and number systems. Compute fluently, and make reasonable estimates.

Objective

Students will demonstrate an understanding of fractional parts of a set and convert fractions to decimals and percentages.

Materials

Tasty Fractions and Percents reproducible
snack-size bags of small, colored candies
calculators (optional)

Strategies

Structured project

Problem-based learning

Your visual/kinesthetic learners will enjoy this edible, hands-on activity while practicing fractions, decimals, and percentages. Have students wash their hands prior to this activity.

1. Show students a bag of small, colored candies. Invite them to brainstorm possible mathematical investigations, and list their suggestions on the board. For example: *What fraction of the candies is yellow? What percent of the candies is yellow? What percent more of the candies is green? What is the ratio of yellow candies to green candies?*

Tasty Fractions and Percents Page 25

2. Students may work individually, in pairs, or in groups based on their ability levels. Distribute a bag of candies and a copy of the **Tasty Fractions and Percents reproducible (page 25)** to students. Have students write at least two predictions about the contents of their bag, using fractions and percentages.

3. Have students complete the table about their bag of candies. They will record the total number of pieces and the frequency of each color. Tell them to use that information to calculate fractions of the whole, decimals of the fractions, and percentages. Encourage

students to reduce fractions to lowest terms, for example *8/40 = 1/5*. Remind them that all the percentages should total 100%.

4. Ask students to write statements to prove or disprove their predictions. Then have them write five math statements about their results, using fractions, decimals, and percentages. For example: *There is 20% more green than yellow.*

5. Pair students with partners to compare their data and write five math statements about it. Encourage them to use inequalities, equivalent fractions, and ratios in their comparisons. For example: *I have 14/50 red, which is < Darren's 12/40 red. The ratio of my red candies to Darren's red candies is 14:12.*

6. Allow each pair to share their information with the class. Invite classmates to evaluate whether the information in the statements are accurate.

Ideas for More Differentiation

Beginning-mastery students may choose to use fewer candies or colors. You may also allow these students to use calculators. For students with a high degree of mastery, include different shapes of candies, as well. Have them determine the fraction and percent of each shape within each color.

Extend the Activity

- Have students write word problems about eating, sharing, or combining their candies. Depending on their ability level, have students include addition, subtraction, multiplication, and division of fractions, decimals, and percentages. Invite students to exchange papers and solve each other's math problems.

- Suggest that students choose and make an appropriate graph to represent their data and explain in writing why they chose that type of graph. Then have them write math problems about their graph for classmates to solve.

- Pose higher-level thinking questions for students to answer. For example: *If you tripled the amount of yellow candies, what percent of the total would be yellow? If you tripled all of the colors, what percent of the total would be yellow?*

Name _____   Date _____

Tasty Fractions and Percents

Directions: Use your bag of candies to answer the questions.

 1. Predict the contents of your bag. Use fractions and percents.

_____

_____

 2. Count and record the total amount in your bag. Complete the table.

Total Amount: _____

Color	Frequency	Fraction	Decimal	Percent

 3. Use your data to prove or disprove your predictions.

_____

_____

4. Analyze your data. On a separate page, write five mathematical statements about it. Include fractions, decimals, and percentages.

 **5.** Compare your data with a classmate's. On a separate page, write five mathematical statements about it. Use inequalities, equivalent fractions, and ratios to help you compare.

Integer Toss

Strategies

Rehearsal

Game

Standard

Numbers and Operations—Compute fluently, and make reasonable estimates.

Objective

Students will practice integer computation.

Materials

chalk

beanbags (various colors)

calculators (optional)

Add an element of novelty to computation practice by having students play a game. Games make computation practice painless and fun. They also allow students to practice math skills thoroughly without even realizing they are practicing! Moreover, games are an excellent communication tool when students discuss the reasons answers are right or wrong. The following game provides practice in adding, subtracting, multiplying, and dividing integers, and it will especially appeal to your bodily/kinesthetic learners. Play this game outside or in a large, open area.

1. Group students according to their level of skill in computing integers. Groups can be any size.

2. Draw a target on the blacktop with chalk for each group. Each target should have three rows and three columns. Write positive and negative integers appropriate for each skill level in each section (e.g., 5, –1, –10, –14, 3, –6, 2, –8, 7).

3. Have the players stand approximately six feet from the target. Rules of the game vary as follows:

Beginning-mastery students focus on one computation skill, such as addition and two integers.

    a. Give each player in the group a different color beanbag.

    b. All players toss their beanbags at the target and get the score of the square in which their beanbag lands.

    c. Players toss their beanbags again and keep a running total of their scores on a sheet of paper.

    d. You can have students can play for a set time, until a set number of games have been played, or until a predetermined number is achieved.

Approaching-mastery students focus on one computation skill and three integers.

    a. Give each student three beanbags of the same color.

    b. All players toss one beanbag at the target and write the integer on a sheet of paper.

    c. Repeat with the other two beanbags and total the scores.

    d. Continue playing, having players keep a running score.

Students with a high degree of mastery focus on two computation skills, such as addition and subtraction, and three integers. The object of the game is to get the lowest (or highest) possible score.

    a. Give each player three beanbags of the same color.

    b. Players toss three beanbags and add and/or subtract the three integers. Players may arrange the integers in any order.

    c. The player with the lowest (or highest) score gets a point. This approach makes students think about how operations affect numbers with opposite values. (You may want to let these students use calculators to check their answers.)

4. Collect all students' score sheets for assessment.

Ideas for More Differentiation

Invite your interpersonal learners to play with a partner. Give each team member the same color beanbag. Team members toss their beanbags and add, subtract, multiply, or divide the two integers to get a team score. They continue tossing their beanbags and keeping a running score for the course of the game.

Algebraic Expressions Match-Up

Standard

Algebra—Represent and analyze mathematical situations and structures using algebraic symbols.

Objective

Students will use variables and appropriate operations to translate phrases into algebraic expressions.

Materials

index cards

marker

The processes of assigning variables to quantities and of translating between verbal and algebraic expressions are fundamental in algebra and higher mathematics. Games are an engaging and motivating way to ensure students get plenty of practice.

1. Write pairs of phrases and algebraic expressions on index cards, one per card. For example: *the square of the quotient of a number and 7, $(n \div 7)^2$; 6 times the sum of a number and 3, $6(n + 3)$; 7 decreased by a number, $7 - n$.* For differentiation, make card sets according to students' readiness levels. For example, some students may require practice with addition and subtraction expressions, while others are ready for square numbers.

2. Expression Match-Up is similar to the game *Concentration*. To play, have students follow these instructions:
   a. Shuffle and lay the cards facedown in a grid format.
   b. Players take turns turning over two cards. If the cards match (phrase and algebraic expression), the player keeps them and gets another turn. If the cards do not match, the player turns them facedown again.
   c. Play until all cards are matched. The player with the most cards wins.

Ideas for More Differentiation

- For more differentiation, have students make two grids with the cards, one with phrases and one with algebraic expressions. Students turn over one card from each grid to find matches.

- Stimulate your bodily/kinesthetic learners with a game of Expression Charades. Place students into groups of two or four. Make a set of phrase cards for each group. One student draws a card and acts out the phrase without speaking. The other students try to guess the phrase. Once students guess the phrase, they write it down in words and translate it into an algebraic expression. Keep playing until each student has had the opportunity to act out the phrase or until no cards remain.

- Engage your verbal/linguistic learners by having them create a crossword puzzle using algebraic expressions and phrases.

- Give each student an expression card. Have them write a real-world situation for the expression. For example, for n + 4: *The Chargers scored four more touchdowns than the Dolphins.*

Equation Crunch

Strategies
Choice board

Rehearsal

Multiple intelligences

Standard
Algebra—Represent and analyze mathematical situations and structures using algebraic symbols.

Objective
Students will solve linear equations.

Materials
Equation Choice Board reproducible

This lesson taps into students' multiple intelligences by providing the opportunity to perform a variety of activities. It also gives students plenty of practice in solving linear equations.

1. Determine if you want students to work individually, with partners, or in groups of three. If students are grouped, assign them based on their level of skill in solving equations.

2. Prior to the activity, write skill-level-appropriate linear equations and numbers on the **Equation Choice Board (page 31)**.

3. Review with the class how to solve equations. Write an equation on the board or chart paper, such as *3x + 2 = 5x*. Solve the equation using manipulatives such as algebra tiles.

4. Distribute the Equation Choice Board reproducible. Allow students to choose activities from the reproducible that they would like to complete. Based on students' abilities, you may want to set a specific number of activities to complete. Have students cross off the box for each completed activity.

5. When students have completed all of their chosen activities, collect their reproducibles and solution papers. These may be used for assessment.

Equation Choice Board Page 31

Name _____   Date _____

Equation Choice Board

Directions: Choose one or more activities to complete.

Write a story problem for this algebraic equation.	Write a poem, song, rap, or jingle explaining how to solve this algebraic equation.	Develop a color code that highlights each step for solving this equation.
Create three linear equations for this number.	Your choice! Get approval from your teacher.	Use manipulatives to solve this algebraic equation. Draw a picture to show each step.
Write a letter to another student explaining how to solve this algebraic equation.	Write an algebraic equation about the picture. Describe how to solve it using the objects on the balance scale. Record your actions symbolically.	Work with a partner to write the steps for solving this algebraic equation.

A New Game!

Strategies

Cooperative group learning

Structured project

Standard

Algebra—Represent and analyze mathematical situations and structures using algebraic symbols.

Objective

Students will develop a game to solve linear equations.

Materials

A New Game! Checklist reproducible
A New Game! Rubric reproducible
A New Game! Reflection reproducible
index cards
paper plates
poster board
art supplies (markers, stickers, rubber stamps, crayons, glue, scissors)
brads
paper clips
dice
plastic disks (or other game markers)

Practice in solving algebraic equations helps students develop fluency and efficiency with higher-level math skills. In this activity, students work in small groups to create a board or card game focused on algebraic equations. This project helps students think about how algebraic equations are written and solved. Allow multiple sessions for students to complete this project.

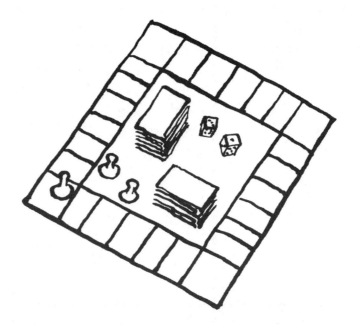

1. Ask students: *What is your favorite game? Why do you like to play it? What makes it fun?* Give students time to think about these questions, and invite them to share their thoughts.

2. Group students heterogeneously, according to their skill levels and learning styles. You may wish to assign roles and duties or allow students to select the roles and duties for which they will be accountable. Roles and duties may include:
   - Production manager—oversees and ensures everyone is working appropriately, encourages other team members, manages conflicts, and facilitates problem solving when necessary.
   - Information manager—ensures the accuracy and quality of the project.
   - Resource manager—gathers and manages the materials necessary to complete the project.
   - Time manager—knows all the deadlines and reminds other group members to stay on task.

3. Give students a copy of the **A New Game! Checklist** and **A New Game! Rubric reproducibles (pages 34–35)** in order to discuss project expectations.

A New Game! Checklist Page 34

4. To help groups in planning and implementing their game idea, list the following questions on the board or chart paper, and discuss:
   - *What are some ways algebraic equations may be used in a game?*
   - *What resources do you have?*
   - *What are the smaller tasks within this big project?*
   - *In what order should we perform the tasks?*
   - *Who will perform each task?*

5. After groups present their games, allow time to play the games. Invite students to give feedback in the form of suggestions, compliments, and constructive criticism. You may wish to write the title of each game on a sheet of chart paper and post each sheet on a bulletin board. Students can write their comments on the appropriate sheets.

6. As a final assessment, have students complete the **A New Game! Reflection reproducible (page 36)**.

A New Game! Reflection Page 36

A New Game! Checklist

Directions: You work for Homegrown Kids Toy Company as a Product Developer. Your team is creating a game for children ages 11–14 that involves solving algebraic equations. The game can be a board game or card game. Your team will present your game to the Selection Committee. Within your presentation, you must give three reasons why the toy company should choose your game.

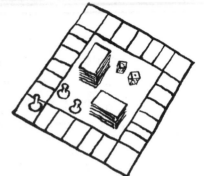

Use this checklist to create your game and presentation. Place a check mark (✔) in the box when the task is complete.

Game Includes

	Game title clearly written on game and instructions
	Age level listed clearly on the instructions
	Organized list of materials to play the game
	Clear, understandable game objectives
	Clear, organized instructions for how to play and win the game
	All pieces to successfully play the game
	A purpose (solving algebraic equations)

Presentation

	Considered the audience and purpose
	Included reasons for creating the new game
	Included three reasons why the toy company should choose the game
	Organized and presented in logical order

Reproducible   978-1-4129-5342-9 • © Corwin Press

Name _____ Date _____

A New Game! Rubric

Directions: Use this rubric to grade students' games and presentations.

Criteria	4	3	2	1
Game Components (title, age level, materials, objective, instructions, game pieces, purpose)	All game components are present, clearly written, well organized, and very neat.	Most game components are present, written, organized, and neat.	Some game components are present, written, organized, and neat.	Incomplete game components are unclear, unorganized, and messy.
Presentation	Presentation effectively matched topic, audience, and purpose.	Presentation was organized and logical.	Some of the presentation was organized.	Presentation did not effectively match the topic, audience, and purpose.
Group Skills	Group always worked well together with all members contributing significant amounts of quality work.	Group generally worked well together with all members contributing some quality of work.	Group worked fairly well together with all members contributing some work.	Group often did not work well together, and game appeared to be the work of one or two people.
Individual Contributions	Successfully completed all of his or her tasks on time; put his or her best effort into creating high-quality work.	Completed most of his or her tasks on time; put effort into creating good work.	Completed some of his or her tasks on time; put some effort into creating the work.	Work was incomplete and seldom on time; put little or no effort into creating the work.

Name _____ Date _____

A New Game! Reflection

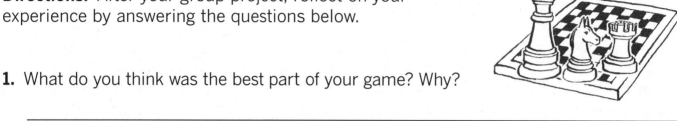

Directions: After your group project, reflect on your
experience by answering the questions below.

1. What do you think was the best part of your game? Why?

_____

_____

2. What did you like best about this project? What would you change?

_____

_____

3. What was your biggest contribution to the creation of your group's game?

_____

_____

4. What problems came up while creating the game, and how did you handle them?

_____

_____

_____

5. After hearing the presentations and playing some of the other group's games,
which games do you think would appeal to most 11- to 14-year-olds? Use examples
to explain your thinking.

_____

_____

_____

_____

_____

Reproducible   978-1-4129-5342-9 • © Corwin Press

What Do You Know?

Standard

Algebra—Understand patterns, relations, and functions.

Objective

Students will develop conceptual understanding of algebraic terms, including patterns and functions.

Pre-assessment is a worthwhile process. It allows teachers to find out what students already know, how they feel about a topic, and what they are interested in learning. Armed with this information, planning for individual needs is easier. The following four-corner pre-assessment may be used to assess a student's prior knowledge about functions. This strategy may also be used to pre-assess students' prior knowledge of other mathematical terms.

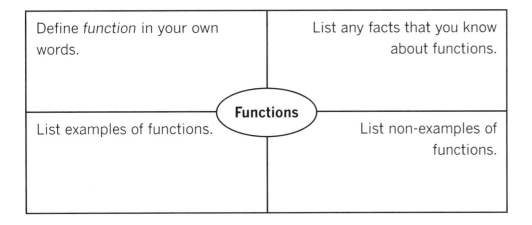

Define *function* in your own words.	List any facts that you know about functions.
List examples of functions.	List non-examples of functions.

(center: **Functions**)

Have students use similar four-quadrant outlines throughout the year as graphic organizers to help them organize mathematical meanings and concepts, to develop a conceptual meaning behind the vocabulary, and to read and use the terms correctly.

Have students make their own organizer by folding a sheet of paper into fourths. Tell them to write the vocabulary word in the center and label the four quadrants *Definition, Facts, Examples,* and *Non-Examples.* Then have them define the word in the first quadrant, write facts about the word in the second, give examples of the word in the third, and write non-examples of the word in the fourth. Students can store their organizers in a binder labeled *Math Vocabulary*.

Mystery Algorithms

Standard
Algebra—Understand patterns, relations, and functions.

Objective
Students will practice developing and solving algorithms.

Materials
calculators

This focus activity opens students' "mental files" to think algebraically and reinforces the concept that the same function can be described by different rules. This activity can be done as a whole class or in small, mixed-ability groups.

1. Divide the class into mixed-ability groups of six. Appoint one student in each group to write a "mystery algorithm" or function rule consisting of one, two, or three steps, for example: *Take a number, multiply it by 2, and add 2* (Rule: *n* x 2 + 2). He or she should not show the algorithm to anyone.

2. Have other group members take turns saying a number to input into the mystery algorithm; the writer responds with the corresponding output. For example: *An input of 3 gives an output of 8* (i.e., 3 x 2 + 2 = 8). Students record inputs and outputs to look for a pattern and identify the mystery algorithm.

Take a number, multiply it by 2, and add 2.

3. If a student thinks he or she knows the algorithm, that student shouts: *Mystery solved!* The student then writes down the algorithm using words or symbols. If the guess is correct, that student becomes the new mystery-algorithm writer. If not, the game continues.

4. If the guess is incorrect, but that student or another student can prove that the algorithm produces the same result as the mystery algorithm, then that is an acceptable answer too. For example, the algorithm rule $(n + 1) \times 2$ produces the same results as the algorithm rule $n \times 2 + 2$.

<table>
<tr><th colspan="2">Rule: $n \times 2 + 2$</th><th colspan="2">Rule: $(n + 1) \times 2$</th></tr>
<tr><th>Input</th><th>Output</th><th>Input</th><th>Output</th></tr>
<tr><td>1</td><td>4</td><td>1</td><td>4</td></tr>
<tr><td>2</td><td>6</td><td>2</td><td>6</td></tr>
<tr><td>3</td><td>8</td><td>3</td><td>8</td></tr>
</table>

5. When students are finished playing the game, have groups share if their functions were the same but described by different rules. Ask them to explain how those algorithms are the same and different, and ask whether or not the graphs would look the same. (Graphically, they should be identical.)

Extend the Activity

For an extension activity, you may choose to have students enter their data in a computer spreadsheet and generate a graph.

Linear Relations in Patterns

Strategies

Lab groups

Journaling

Standards

Algebra—Understand patterns, relations, and functions.

Represent and analyze mathematical situations and structures using algebraic symbols.

Use mathematical models to represent and understand quantitative relationships.

Analyze change in various contexts.

Objective

Students will work together to generalize pattern through function and equation and explore relationships between symbolic expressions and graphs of lines.

Materials

Cuisenaire® rods

resealable plastic bags

graph paper

centimeter rulers

calculators

Functions are all around us. Algebraic tools help students to visually express these functional relationships so they can grasps the magnitude, direction, and rate of change between the variables. This activity uses concrete materials to see how a pattern grows, while students explore the concepts of linear function and slope. Through group learning, students use inductive and deductive reasoning to formulate mathematical arguments.

1. Separate the colors of Cuisenaire® rods into resealable plastic bags. (Note that each color represents a different length.) Divide the class into mixed-ability groups of three or four, and give a bag of rods and graph paper to each group.

2. Describe the following tasks to students:
   - *Calculate the surface area of one rod, two rods, three rods, and up to ten rods. Place the longest sides of rods together to determine the surface area of more than one rod. Create a table.*
   - *Look for a pattern, and use words to write a rule.*
   - *Generate a formula for the nth rod.*
   - *Graph your data. Write a title and labels.*

For example, using the ten-unit color rods, students should calculate the following:

# Rods	Surface Area per Face	Total Surface Area
1	Top and bottom: (1 x 10) x 2 = 20 Front and back: (1 x 10) x 2 = 20 Both ends: (1 x 1) x 2 = 2	42 units
2	Top and bottom: (2 x 10) x 2 = 40 Front and back: (1 x 10) x 2 = 20 Both ends: (1 x 2) x 2 = 4	64 units
3	Top and bottom: (3 x 10) x 2 = 60 Front and back: (1 x 10) x 2 = 20 Both ends: (1 x 3) x 2 = 6	86 units

You may choose to have students use a computer to record their data in a spreadsheet and make a graph.

3. Circulate among the groups, listening and asking guiding questions such as:
   - *Do you see a pattern as you look down the surface area column?*
   - *Look at the stack from different angles. What do you notice? What do you notice about the surface area from each angle?*
   - *What are the variables in this situation? What quantities are changing?*

4. Have students write in their journals to reflect on their participation and learning. Prompt students with questions such as: *Did working as a group make your work easier or harder? Write three things you learned today.*

Ideas for More Differentiation

Develop a three-tiered activity, and group students according to readiness levels. For beginning mastery, eliminate the graphing. For approaching mastery, have students complete the activity as written. For high degree of mastery, have students find the volume for the rods, make a graph, and compare and contrast the graphs.

Polynomial Puzzles

Strategies
Multiple intelligences

Presentation

Standards
Algebra—Understand patterns, relations, and functions.

Represent and analyze mathematical situations and structures using algebraic symbols.

Use mathematical models to represent and understand quantitative relationships.

Objective
Students will create visual models and algebraic expressions of polynomials.

Materials
1" grid paper

transparencies and markers

colored pencils

scissors

glue

white construction paper

paper clips

Because of their simple structure, polynomials are often used in the analysis of patterns and relationships among variables. In this activity, students use colored shapes to model polynomial terms. This approach appeals especially to visual/spatial and logical/mathematical learners.

1. In advance, make several transparencies of 1" grid paper. Review with students the definition of *polynomial* (an algebraic expression of one or more terms added together, written in decreasing order by exponents). Remind students that polynomials with one term, such as $2x^2$, are called *monomials*; two-term polynomials, such as $2x^2 + 4$, are called *binomials*; three-term polynomials, such as $2x^2 + 5x + 4$, are called *trinomials*; and so on.

2. Write a polynomial on the board. Invite students to name the polynomial; underline the terms; and identify each variable, coefficient, and constant. Repeat with more examples.

3. Use a grid paper transparency to demonstrate how to represent the polynomial $2x^2 + 5x + 4$ with colored rectangles. Display and use the following Construction Guide:

Construction Guide
- For each constant term (numeral only), use 1" x 1" squares.
- For each x, use a 1" x 3" rectangle.
- For each x^2, use a 3" x 3" square.
- Use a different color for each of the three shapes.
- Write a + symbol to represent a positive value or addition and a – symbol to represent a negative value or subtraction.

4. Have volunteers arrange the shapes. (Show two 3" x 3" squares, five 1" x 3" rectangles, and four 1" x 1" squares, all with + written on them.) Write the polynomial below them. Repeat with examples of subtraction and negative values, such as $-3x^2 - 6$.

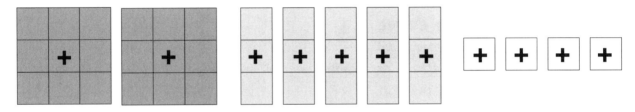

$$2x^2 + 5x + 4$$

5. Give students grid paper and white construction paper to make models using the Construction Guide and the following directions:
   - Write a polynomial lengthwise along the bottom of the construction paper.
   - Follow the Construction Guide. Draw, color, cut out, and glue shapes from the grid paper to make a model of the polynomial.
   - Fold up the bottom of the construction paper to hide the polynomial from view. Use a paperclip to close the flap.
   - Invite classmates to look at the model and try to guess the polynomial. Then open the flap to show if they are correct.

Ideas for More Differentiation
- Have beginning mastery students focus only on monomials, binomials, and positive terms. Provide them with pre-drawn shapes to cut out and write the corresponding polynomial.

- Have high degree mastery students model and solve trinomial addition problems, combining like terms, removing neutral pairs (those that cancel each other), and writing the solution. For example: $(3x^2 + 2x + 5) + (2x^2 - 3x - 1) = 5x^2 - x + 4$.

CHAPTER 3

Geometry

Interior Angles of Polygons

Strategies

Jigsaw

Journaling

Standard

Geometry—Analyze characteristics and properties of two- and three-dimensional geometric shapes, and develop mathematical arguments about geometric relationships.

Objective

Students will investigate interior angles of polygons and discover an algebraic formula for determining the sum of the interior angles of any polygon.

Materials

Interior Angles of Polygons reproducibles
Interior Angles of Polygons Table reproducible
scissors
drawing paper
colored pencils
rulers

Jigsaw is an effective strategy to enhance learning and increase retention and interdependence. In this activity, students share responsibility for determining the sum of the measures of interior angles. They also discover algebraic formulas by dividing polygons into triangles from one vertex. The movement and interaction among classmates stimulates both intra- and interpersonal learners.

1. Draw a triangle on the board, and review with students that the sum of the interior angles of any triangle is 180°. Tell students that they will use this information to explore the sum of the interior angles of other polygons by dividing polygons into triangles.

2. Demonstrate on the board how to divide a regular convex polygon, an irregular convex polygon, and a concave polygon into triangles by drawing diagonals to connect one vertex to all of the others.

978-1-4129-5342-9

Have students refer to these examples when dividing their polygons.

Regular Convex Polygon
(regular pentagon)
all sides equal

Irregular Convex Polygon
(irregular pentagon)
sides unequal

Irregular Concave Polygon
(irregular pentagon)
sides unequal

3. Divide the class into mixed-ability groups of six (base groups). Give each group both **Interior Angles of Polygons reproducibles (pages 46– 47)**. Have them cut apart the reproducibles and give one section to each group member.

4. Have students with the same polygon form an expert group and complete their section (e.g., pentagons work together). First, students independently draw their polygon and use a colored pencil and ruler to divide it into triangles. Expert-group members then compare and contrast their drawings and complete the information.

5. After students finish working with their expert groups, base groups reconvene to share information. Have each group complete the **Polygon Angles Table reproducible (page 48)**.

6. For assessment, have students write in their journals. Prompt them with questions such as:
   - *What is the formula for calculating the number of triangles formed from a polygon, given n = the number of sides? (n – 2) What is the formula for calculating the sum of the measures of its interior angles? [(n – 2) x 180°]*
   - *How many triangles can be drawn from one vertex of a 53-sided polygon? (51) Explain how you found your answer. [(n – 2) = (53 – 2) = 51 triangles]*
   - *What is the sum of the interior angle measures of a 20-sided polygon? (3,240°) Explain your answer. [(n – 2) = (20 – 2) = 18 triangles, so 18 x 180° = 3,240°]*
   - *How many sides does a polygon have if the sum of its interior angle measures is 2,340°? (15 sides; 2,340°/180° = 13 triangles, so 13 + 2 = 15 sides)*

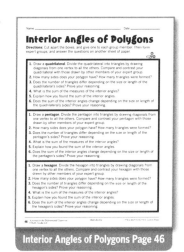

Interior Angles of Polygons Page 46

Polygon Angles Table Page 48

Interior Angles of Polygons

Directions: Cut apart the boxes, and give one to each group member. Then form expert groups, and answer the questions on another sheet of paper.

1. Draw a **quadrilateral**. Divide the quadrilateral into triangles by drawing diagonals from one vertex to all the others. Compare and contrast your quadrilateral with those drawn by other members of your expert group.
2. How many sides does your polygon have? How many triangles were formed?
3. Does the number of triangles differ depending on the size or length of the quadrilateral's sides? Prove your reasoning.
4. What is the sum of the measures of the interior angles?
5. Explain how you found the sum of the interior angles.
6. Does the sum of the interior angles change depending on the size or length of the quadrilateral's sides? Prove your reasoning.

---

1. Draw a **pentagon**. Divide the pentagon into triangles by drawing diagonals from one vertex to all the others. Compare and contrast your pentagon with those drawn by other members of your expert group.
2. How many sides does your polygon have? How many triangles were formed?
3. Does the number of triangles differ depending on the size or length of the pentagon's sides? Prove your reasoning.
4. What is the sum of the measures of the interior angles?
5. Explain how you found the sum of the interior angles.
6. Does the sum of the interior angles change depending on the size or length of the pentagon's sides? Prove your reasoning.

---

1. Draw a **hexagon**. Divide the hexagon into triangles by drawing diagonals from one vertex to all the others. Compare and contrast your hexagon with those drawn by other members of your expert group.
2. How many sides does your polygon have? How many triangles were formed?
3. Does the number of triangles differ depending on the size or length of the hexagon's sides? Prove your reasoning.
4. What is the sum of the measures of the interior angles?
5. Explain how you found the sum of the interior angles.
6. Does the sum of the interior angles change depending on the size or length of the hexagon's sides? Prove your reasoning.

Interior Angles of Polygons

Directions: Cut apart the boxes, and give one to each group member. Then form expert groups, and answer the questions on another sheet of paper.

---

1. Draw a **heptagon**. Divide the heptagon into triangles by drawing diagonals from one vertex to all the others. Compare and contrast your heptagon with those drawn by other members of your expert group.
2. How many sides does your polygon have? How many triangles were formed?
3. Does the number of triangles differ depending on the size or length of the heptagon's sides? Prove your reasoning.
4. What is the sum of the measures of the interior angles?
5. Explain how you found the sum of the interior angles.
6. Does the sum of the interior angles change depending on the size or length of the heptagon's sides? Prove your reasoning.

---

1. Draw an **octagon**. Divide the octagon into triangles by drawing diagonals from one vertex to all the others. Compare and contrast your octagon with those drawn by other members of your expert group.
2. How many sides does your polygon have? How many triangles were formed?
3. Does the number of triangles differ depending on the size or length of the octagon's sides? Prove your reasoning.
4. What is the sum of the measures of the interior angles?
5. Explain how you found the sum of the interior angles.
6. Does the sum of the interior angles change depending on the size or length of the octagon's sides? Prove your reasoning.

---

1. Draw a **nonagon**. Divide the nonagon into triangles by drawing diagonals from one vertex to all the others. Compare and contrast your nonagon with those drawn by other members of your expert group.
2. How many sides does your polygon have? How many triangles were formed?
3. Does the number of triangles differ depending on the size or length of the nonagon's sides? Prove your reasoning.
4. What is the sum of the measures of the interior angles?
5. Explain how you found the sum of the interior angles.
6. Does the sum of the interior angles change depending on the size or length of the nonagon's sides? Prove your reasoning.

Polygon Angles Table

Directions: As a group, complete the table and answer the questions.

Polygon Name	Number of Sides	Number of Triangles Formed	Sum of the Measures of Interior Angles
Triangle	3	1	180°
Quadrilateral			
Pentagon			
Hexagon			
Heptagon			
Octagon			
Nonagon			

1. What is the relationship between the number of a polygon's sides and the number of triangles formed? Express your answer in words and as an algebraic expression.

   _____

   _____

2. What happens to the number of triangles when another side is added to a polygon?

   _____

3. Look for a pattern(s) in the table. What do you observe? Explain.

   _____

4. Based on the patterns, into how many triangles can an 18-sided polygon be divided? What is the sum of the interior angle measures?

   _____

5. Based on the information from #4, write an algebraic formula for finding the sum of the interior angles of a polygon with *n* sides.

   _____

         978-1-4129-5342-9 • © Corwin Press

Geometry Battleship

Standard

Geometry—Specify locations and describe spatial relationships using coordinate geometry and other representational systems.

Objective

Students will identify and plot geometric shapes using ordered pairs on a coordinate grid.

Materials

coordinate grid paper
transparency and markers
file or pocket folders
rulers
colored pencils

This game is similar to *Battleship*® and allows students to practice coordinate graphing as well as naming geometric shapes. Students will use logic to find the hidden shapes.

1. Show students a transparency of coordinate grid paper, and review how to plot ordered pairs in each of the four quadrants. Invite students to help plot the points. Connect some of the points to show polygons.

2. Give each student two coordinate grid papers. Pair students by ability levels, and have partners sit across from each other or next to each other. Have them prop up a file or pocket folder between them so they can't see each other's papers. Tell students that they are going to play a geometric version of the game *Battleship*®.

3. Have each player use a ruler and pencil to draw four geometric shapes on one of their coordinate grids. The shapes must be at least 1" high and 1" wide; they cannot touch each other; and all vertices must be drawn at intersection points of the grid lines (not in between the lines or between the numbers).

4. Partners may choose to play "Plane Geometry Battleshapes" (drawing four different polygons) or

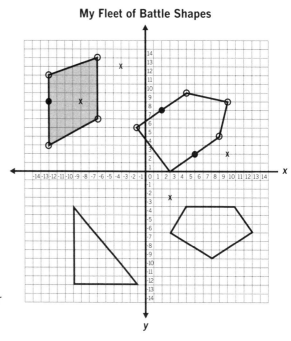

My Fleet of Battle Shapes

"Solid Geometry Battleshapes" (drawing three-dimensional shapes).

5. Have students title their grid of shapes *My Fleet of Battleshapes*. Have them title their other, blank coordinate grid *My Opponent's Fleet*. Tell them to place both papers side by side on their desk.

6. To play the game, have students follow these directions:

   a. Players take turns calling out ordered pairs to try and locate the vertices of their partner's hidden shapes.

   b. Players say *hit* or *miss* after each of their partner's guesses, marking an *O* for a hit or an *X* for a miss at each point on their *My Fleet of Battleshapes* grid. Likewise, their partner draws an *O* or an *X* at that point on his or her *My Opponent's Fleet* grid, tracking progress in locating the hidden shapes.

   c. If a player names a point on the side of the shape but not the vertex, the partner says *side swipe* and marks the point as a solid dot instead of *O* or *X*.

   d. When a player successfully hits the last vertex of a shape, the partner says *hit and sunk*, coloring his or her sunken shape on the *My Fleet of Battleshapes* grid. Meanwhile, the player connects all the points on his or her *My Opponent's Fleet* grid to show the discovered shape's location, and writes the name of that shape inside of it.

   e. To win the game, players must correctly locate, draw, and name all of their opponent's shapes. If students are not sure of the names, encourage them to check a math textbook before showing the grid to their partner.

My Opponent's Fleet

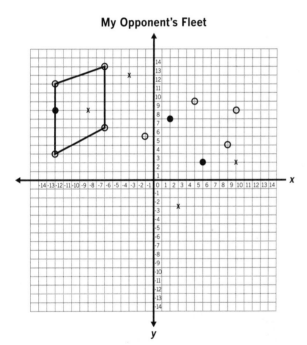

Ideas for More Differentiation

- Have beginning-mastery students draw only two or three shapes. You might also have them use regular grid paper and only positive numbers.

- Instead of playing a game, partners can make duplicate drawings by calling out the ordered pairs of vertices of secretly drawn shapes. They mark the points on their grids, connect the points to draw the shapes, and then name the shapes.

Quadrilateral Shapes

Standard
Geometry—Analyze characteristics and properties of two- and three-dimensional geometric shapes, and develop mathematical arguments about geometric relationships.

Strategy
Graphic organizer

Objective
Students will use graphic organizers to understand the basic properties of and relationships pertaining to quadrilaterals.

Materials
Special Quadrilaterals reproducible
Quadrilateral Relationships reproducible
transparencies and marker

Understanding relationships of special quadrilaterals and using inductive reasoning is the foundation of understanding and articulating higher geometric and mathematical concepts. Graphic organizers help students visualize the relationships between the types of quadrilaterals, making it easier to develop inductive arguments concerning geometric ideas and relationships.

1. Prior to the activity, make transparencies of the **Special Quadrilaterals** and **Quadrilateral Relationships reproducibles (pages 54–55)**.

2. Review the definition of a general quadrilateral (*polygon with four sides*). Have students name items in our world that are quadrilaterals (e.g., *computer screen, television, basketball court, book, desktop*).

3. Display the Special Quadrilaterals transparency, and give each student a photocopy. Have students identify the properties of each quadrilateral.

4. Next, display the Quadrilateral Relationships transparency, and give each student a photocopy. Review the relationship of overlapping sets overlap, sets that do not overlap, and sets entirely inside other sets.

5. Tell students that, based on these properties and definitions, they will complete a Venn diagram to show the relationships between these types of quadrilaterals. This activity can be done as a class, in small groups or pairs, or individually, depending on students' ability levels.

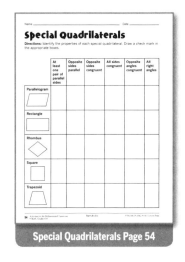

Special Quadrilaterals Page 54

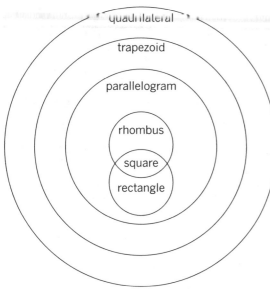

6. Have students write the name of the quadrilateral, draw a picture of the shape, and then justify their answer. For example:

- *A rhombus is a quadrilateral with four congruent sides. A parallelogram is a quadrilateral with opposite sides parallel. Since opposite sides of a rhombus are parallel to one another, a rhombus is a special kind of parallelogram.*

- *A rectangle is a subset of a parallelogram. A rectangle has all the properties of a parallelogram with one additional property of four right angles. You can't make a rectangle that is not a parallelogram.*

Note: The Venn diagram will vary depending on the definitions used. For example: *Trapezoid—(1) quadrilateral with at least one pair of parallel sides; or (2) exactly one pair of parallel sides.* The first definition is used for the Venn diagram shown here.

7. Prompt students to analyze the relationships between quadrilaterals. For example: *Is a square always, sometimes, or never a rectangle?* (always) Ask students to explain their reasoning. For example: *A square is always a rectangle because it has all the properties of a rectangle and all sides are congruent.*

Ideas for More Differentiation

- Have beginning-mastery students draw Venn diagrams using fewer special quadrilaterals (e.g., rectangle and square or parallelograms; rhombus, rectangle, and square).

- Have high-mastery students add kite and isosceles trapezoids to their Venn diagrams, or have them draw their own Venn diagrams (not use the reproducible). They can write their own true/false statements and explain their reasoning.

- Invite your bodily/kinesthetic learners to make a Venn diagram on the floor, using string and name/definition cards. Each student represents a certain quadrilateral and stands in the appropriate section of the diagram. Each "shape" then makes a true and a false statement about him or herself.

• Create a choice board such as the following:

Write a story about the relationships between the quadrilaterals.	Create a song or poem about the relationships between the quadrilaterals.	Design a game to increase understanding of the mathematical arguments about geometric relationships.
Design a poster or cartoon strip to show the relationships between the quadrilaterals.	Create a puppet show to show the relationships between quadrilaterals.	Interview someone about his or her understanding of the quadrilateral relationships. Record or videotape your interview.
Pretend you are a square. Explain how you are related to a parallelogram, rectangle, and rhombus.	Collect a variety of pictures showing the uses of quadrilaterals in everyday life.	Design an original work of art using quadrilaterals. Present it to the class.

Extend the Activity

Give each student two index cards. Have students write *true* on one card and *false* on the other. Display the Special Quadrilaterals transparency. Tell students that you will say a statement about quadrilaterals. In response, they will hold up one card, showing whether the statement is true or false. Possible statements:

• *A parallelogram is never a square.* (false)

• *Every square is a rectangle.* (true)

• *A rhombus is never a square.* (false)

• *A trapezoid is always a quadrilateral.* (true)

• *A rectangle is a square.* (false)

• *Every square is a rhombus.* (true)

Name _____   Date _____

Special Quadrilaterals

Directions: Identify the properties of each special quadrilateral. Draw a check mark in the appropriate boxes.

	At least one pair of parallel sides	Opposite sides parallel	Opposite sides congruent	All sides congruent	Opposite angles congruent	All right angles
Parallelogram						
Rectangle						
Rhombus						
Square						
Trapezoid						

Reproducible   978-1-4129-5342-9 • © Corwin Press

Name _____ Date _____

Quadrilateral Relationships

Directions: Write the quadrilateral name, and draw a picture in the appropriate section of the Venn diagram to show the relationships between the quadrilaterals.

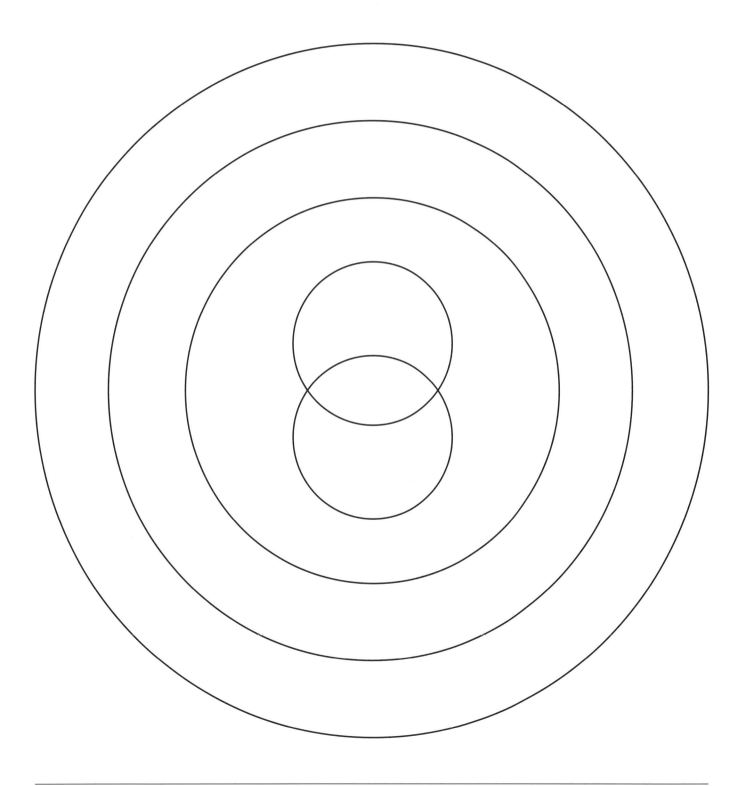

A Human Circle

Strategies

Focus activity

Role play

Standard

Geometry—Analyze characteristics and properties of two- and three-dimensional geometric shapes, and develop mathematical arguments about geometric relationships.

Objective

Students will create a human circle to review the parts of a circle.

Materials

yarn

compasses and rulers

This focus activity will get students thinking about the parts of a circle, as well as give them the opportunity to get up and move around! Students must have a thorough understanding of circles in order to continue with more advanced concepts, such as measuring the circumference, area, and central angles.

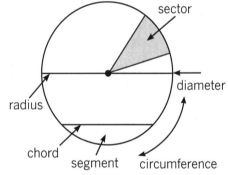

1. Have students stand in a circle outdoors. Ask: *What shape have we formed?* (circle) *What is the distance around the circle called?* (circumference) Invite a volunteer to sit in the exact middle of the circle to be the "center."

2. Give a length of yarn to two "circumference" students standing opposite each other. Have them stretch the yarn across the circle, passing through (over) the center. Have the class identify the circle part. (*diameter*)

3. Continue to form and identify other parts of a circle, including chords, radii, sectors, arcs, central angles, and secants. Use new volunteers for the center.

4. When you're back in the classroom, have students use a compass to draw and label a diagram showing the parts of a circle they modeled outside.

Ideas for More Differentiation

While outdoors, assign each student a different letter of the alphabet, assigning the letter *C* to the "center" volunteer. Have students use those letters to name each part of the circle they identify and model. For example: *Radius AC or CA.*

Tricky Triangles Game

Standard
Geometry—Analyze characteristics and properties of two- and three-dimensional geometric shapes, and develop mathematical arguments about geometric relationships.

Objective
Students will play a game to classify triangles according to their attributes.

Materials
Tricky Triangles Game Cards reproducibles
cardstock
scissors
resealable plastic bags

Strategies
Rehearsal

Game

Triangles are the most-used figures in geometry and fields beyond, such as engineering; so it's important for students to understand and identify triangles. What better way to practice than with a game! This game provides a fun, motivational way for students to practice their knowledge of the "tricky triangle."

1. Prior to the activity, reproduce the **Tricky Triangle Game Cards (pages 59–61)** onto cardstock. Make a set for each student and cut them apart. Students can store cards in resealable plastic bags.

2. Review with students that a triangle can be classified in two ways—by its sides and by its angles. Tell students that they will play a version of the card game *Rummy*; in this variation, they will classify triangles by both sides and angles. The object of the game is to gather sets of three or four cards that describe the same type of triangle—name card (e.g., *isosceles, acute triangle*), picture card, and two description cards (e.g., *two sides are equal, all three angles are less than 90°*).

3. Groups students in pairs or groups of three according to their level of skill in classifying triangles. They may either play the 7-card version or the 11-card version. If they play in groups of three or play the 11-card version, they must use two decks of cards. Explain and demonstrate the rules of the game as follows:
    a. The dealer gives each player 7 (or 11) cards. He or she places the remaining stack facedown on the table, turns over the

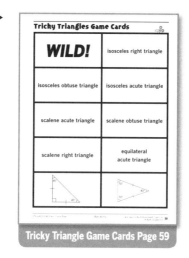

Tricky Triangle Game Cards Page 59

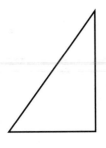

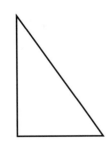

top card, and places it face up next to the deck to begin the discard pile.

b. Players hold their cards out of their opponents' view. They begin by putting down any card sets they have for each type of triangle.

c. Players take turns choosing a card from either the deck or the discard pile. If players choose to keep the new card, they must discard one of their other cards.

d. The object of the game is to be the first player to put all of his or her cards into complete sets and lay them on the table. During a turn, players can put down sets of three or four cards at a time. They may also add a fourth card to a set of three. The cards in each set must describe the same type of triangle. If a player gets the *Wild!* card, he or she may use it with any card set.

e. If players go through the entire deck before anyone wins, the dealer shuffles the discard pile to form the deck again, turning over the top card to start another discard pile. The first player to correctly use all of his or her cards in sets wins the game.

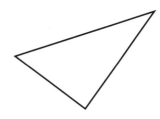

Ideas for More Differentiation

- Provide a reference sheet that shows each type of triangle along with its name and description. Encourage students to refer to this sheet as they play the game.

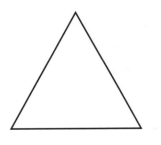

- Have high-degree mastery students modify the game by including additional cards about triangles or other polygons. They may also make a more advanced deck of cards about geometry, using themes such as: classifying quadrilaterals, matching shapes by perimeter or area (including the Pythagorean theorem), supplementary angles and interior angles, arcs of circles, classifying solid figures (including nets), or matching solid figures with the same volume.

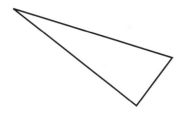

- Use the cards for one-on-one instruction with students who need extra support. For example, review that the sum of the measures of any triangle's angles is 180°; find the measure of missing angles; using picture cards, have students tell how the triangles are alike (e.g., *all have three sides, all have three angles, the angles add up to 180°*).

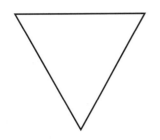

WILD!	isosceles right triangle
isosceles obtuse triangle	isosceles acute triangle
scalene acute triangle	scalene obtuse triangle
scalene right triangle	equilateral acute triangle
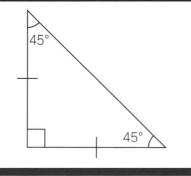	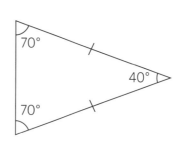

Tricky Triangles Game Cards

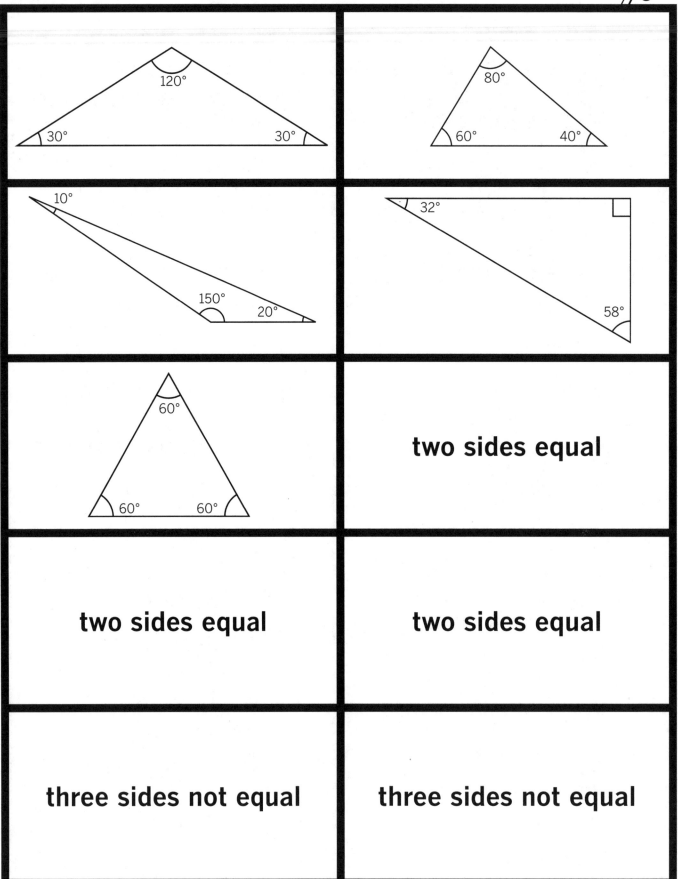

two sides equal

two sides equal

two sides equal

three sides not equal

three sides not equal

Reproducible   978-1-4129-5342-9 • © *Corwin Press*

Tricky Triangles Game Cards

three sides not equal	three sides equal
three angles less than 90°	three angles less than 90°
three angles less than 90°	one angle 90°
one angle 90°	one angle 90°
one angle more than 90°	one angle more than 90°

Colorful Angles and Transversals

Strategy

Jigsaw

Standard

Geometry—Analyze characteristics and properties of two- and three-dimensional geometric shapes, and develop mathematical arguments about geometric relationships.

Objective

Students will color-code angles to identify those formed by parallel lines cut by a transversal.

Materials

Angles/Transversals Diagram reproducible
Angles/Transversals Guide reproducibles
12" x 18" or 9" x 12" construction paper
different colored dot stickers
different colored markers
protractors
scissors

Students often get confused as they try to identify angles formed when two parallel lines are cut by a transversal. A simple method to help students identify these angles is to color-code and use letter-shape visuals. This strategy especially appeals to visual/spatial learners.

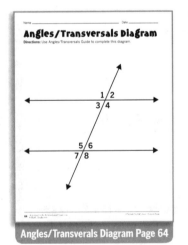

Angles/Transverals Diagram Page 64

1. Give each student a protractor and a copy of the **Angles/ Transversals Diagram reproducible (page 64)**. Review the terms *adjacent, complimentary,* and *supplementary* by using Angles 1, 2, 3, and 4 in the diagram. For example, ask students: *Are Angle 1 and Angle 2 adjacent angles? How do you know?* (Yes; they share a common side.) *Are they complimentary or supplementary angles? How do you know?* (Supplementary; they form a straight angle, and the sum of their measures is 180°.) Model how to use a protractor to measure the angles as students follow along on their own diagrams.

2. Explain to students that a *transversal* is a line that crosses two parallel lines, as shown in the diagram. Explain that the term *interior* means "between the two parallel lines," *exterior* means "outside the parallel lines," and *alternate* means "alternating sides of the transversal." Point out several examples in the diagram.

3. Divide the class into mixed-ability groups of six. These are the base groups. Give each base group a copy of the **Angles/Transversals Guide reproducibles (pages 65–66)** and different colored markers and dot stickers (about six per color for each student). Have students cut apart the sections of their guide and give one section to each group member, along with four colors of dots.

Angles/Transversals Guide Page 65

4. Tell students with the same angles to form expert groups, working together to complete their diagrams (e.g., vertical angles work together, alternate interior angles work together). Monitor groups as they work, and offer assistance as needed. Remind students to place dot stickers next to numbers in the angles, not on top, so they can name the angles (e.g., name <2 and <3 *acute vertical angles*). Urge them to turn their diagrams to view different layouts more easily.

5. After students complete their diagrams, have them go back to their base groups and share what they've learned. Ask students to form partners within their group, exchange diagrams, and take turns asking each other questions such as: *What types of angles are shown in my diagram? What are the names of the matching pairs? Which angles are congruent? How do you know?* Then have students rotate partners and repeat the process with another group member. Continue until everyone in the group has seen all the diagrams.

6. Conclude the activity by having groups bind their diagrams together in a construction paper cover to make booklets. File booklets for student reference.

Extend the Activity

Have students write statements and expressions about their completed diagrams. For example: *<1 = <8 because they are alternate exterior angles. Consecutive interior angles are supplementary, so <1 + <2 = 180°.* You might also have students use letters to label the vertices and other points of their angles so they can use the three-letter naming system. For example: *<ABC = <DBE because they are alternate exterior angles.* Point out that the vertex is always written in the middle.

Angles/Transversals Diagram

Directions: Use Angles/Transversals Guide to complete this diagram.

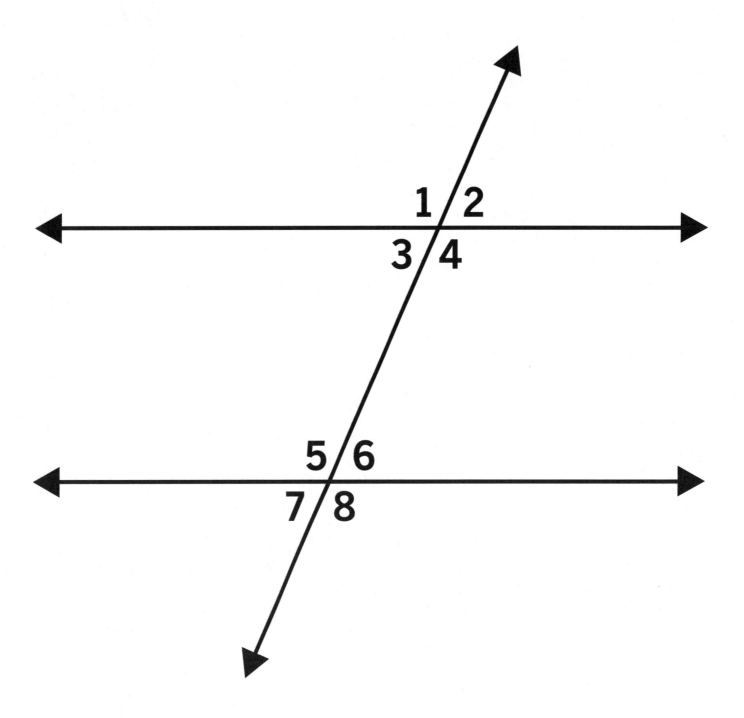

Angles/Transversals Guide

Directions: Cut out the boxes, and give one to each group member. Complete your diagram as instructed. Answer the questions on another sheet of paper.

Vertical Angles are opposite angles formed when two lines intersect, as shown.

1. Use matching, colored dots to show the vertical angles in your diagram. Use a different color for each pair. How many pairs are there?

2. How many pairs are **acute** vertical angles?

3. How many pairs are **obtuse** vertical angles?

4. Use a protractor to measure each pair of vertical angles. Record your results.

5. What do you notice about the measurements? Discuss and record your findings.

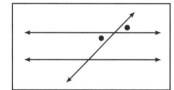

Alternate Interior Angles are pairs of interior angles that lie on opposite sides of a transversal and along different parallel lines, as shown.

1. Find the zigzag Z shape in your diagram. Use a colored marker to trace it. Put matching, colored dots in the two angles inside the Z.

2. Use a protractor to measure the alternate interior angles. Record your results.

3. Now find the backward Z shape. Use a different colored marker to trace it. Put another color of matching dots in the two angles inside the backward Z.

4. Use a protractor to measure the alternate interior angles. Record your results.

5. What do you notice about the measurements? Discuss and record your findings.

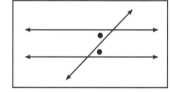

Alternate Exterior Angles are pairs of exterior angles that lie on opposite sides of a transversal and along different parallel lines, as shown.

1. Find the zigzag Z shape in your diagram. Use a colored marker to trace it. Put matching, colored dots in the two outer angles of the Z, above and below.

2. Use a protractor to measure the alternate exterior angles. Record your results.

3. Now find the backward Z shape. Use a different colored marker to trace it. Put another color of matching dots in the two outer angles of the backward Z.

4. Use a protractor to measure the alternate exterior angles. Record your results.

5. What do you notice about the measurements? Discuss and record your findings.

Name _____ Date _____

Angles/Transversals Guide

Directions: Cut out the boxes, and give one to each group member. Complete your diagram as instructed. Answer the questions on another sheet of paper.

Corresponding Angles are any pair of angles that have the same relative position at each intersection where a transversal crosses parallel lines, as shown.

1. Find the *F* shape in your diagram. Use a colored marker to trace it. Put matching, colored dots inside the two corners of the *F*.

2. Measure and record the corresponding angles. Repeat for the pair of corresponding angles above the corners of the *F*.

3. Now find the backward *F* shape. Use a different colored marker to trace it. Put another color of matching dots inside the two corners of the backward *F*.

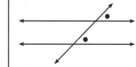

4. Use a protractor to measure the corresponding angles. Record your results.

5. Repeat for the pair of corresponding angles above the corners of the backward *F*.

6. Discuss and record your findings.

Consecutive Interior Angles are interior angles lying on the same side of a transversal cutting across two parallel lines, as shown.

1. Find the right-facing *U* shape in your diagram. Use a colored marker to trace it. Put matching, colored dots in the two angles inside the *U*. Measure and record the interior angles.

2. Now find the left-facing U shape. Use a different-colored marker to trace it. Put another color of matching dots in the two angles inside it.

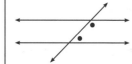

3. Measure the interior angles. Record your results.

4. Discuss and record your findings.

Consecutive Exterior Angles are exterior angles lying on the same side of a transversal cutting across two parallel lines, as shown.

1. Find the right-facing *U* shape in your diagram. Use a colored marker to trace it. Put matching, colored dots in the outer angles above and below the *U*.

2. Use a protractor to measure the exterior angles. Record your results.

3. Now find the left-facing *U* shape. Use a different colored marker to trace it. Put another color of dots in the two outer angles above and below.

4. Measure the exterior angles. Record your results.

5. Discuss and record your findings.

978-1-4129-5342-9 • © Corwin Press

Show the Shapes

Standards

Geometry—Analyze characteristics and properties of two- and three-dimensional geometric shapes, and develop mathematical arguments about geometric relationships.

Measurement—Understand measurable attributes of objects and the units, systems, and processes of measurement.

Apply appropriate techniques, tools, and formulas to determine measurements.

Strategies
Center activity

Adjustable project

Objective

Students will construct, measure, and describe two- and three-dimensional shapes.

Geometric shapes are all around us. Plane figures such as triangles and quadrilaterals are often found in both natural and human-made patterns. Solid figures, such as cubes, rectangular prisms, cylinders, and pyramids, are commonly used shapes for household containers and are often incorporated into buildings and structures throughout the world. The following center activities provide hands-on practice for students to create and explore two- and three-dimensional shapes. Students may work in pairs or individually, depending on their ability levels.

Center 1: Plane Figures

Materials: index cards (three colors), plastic coffee stirrers, protractors, metric rulers, scissors, glue bottles, cardstock, yarn

1. Prior to the activity, color-code index cards according to students' readiness levels (beginning mastery, approaching mastery, high degree of mastery). Make card sets with descriptions of triangles and quadrilaterals. For example:
   - *triangle with two congruent sides, one right angle* (right, isosceles)
   - *triangle with no congruent sides, three angles less than 90°* (acute, scalene)
   - *triangle with all congruent sides, three angles less than 90°* (acute, equilateral)
   - *triangle with two congruent sides, one angle greater than 90°* (obtuse, isosceles)
   - *quadrilateral with four congruent sides, four congruent angles* (square)

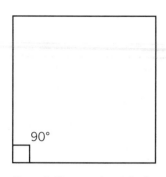

Quadrilateral with four congruent sides and four congruent angles

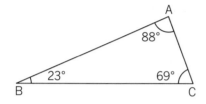

Triangle with no sides congruent, three angles less than 90°: 23°, 88°, 69°

- quadrilateral with four congruent sides but not four congruent angles (rhombus)
- quadrilateral with four congruent angles but not four congruent sides (rectangle)
- quadrilateral with no congruent sides, no congruent angles (irregular quadrilateral)
- quadrilateral with two pairs of parallel sides, four right angles (rectangle, square)
- quadrilateral with four congruent sides, four right angles (square)
- quadrilateral with at least one pair of parallel sides (parallelogram, trapezoid, rhombus, square, rectangle)

2. Place the materials at a center along with the cards, and give students the following instructions: *Choose several cards, and create the shapes by cutting pieces of coffee stirrers and gluing them onto cardstock. Use a protractor and ruler as needed. Label each figure with its name, description, and measurements.*

Ideas for More Differentiation

Instead of using coffee stirrers, students may use protractors to draw each shape and then use glue and yarn to trace around each figure. Invite them to predict the amount of yarn needed for each shape, using the perimeter and area. They can check by measuring the yarn as they use it.

Extend the Activity

- Have students prove that opposite sides of congruent angles are also congruent.

- Have students with a high degree of mastery also calculate perimeter and area. Have them use algebraic equations to describe the sides, angles, perimeter, and area of each shape. For example: *If the sides of a rectangle are labeled 2x, x, 2x, x, the perimeter is 2x + 2x + x + x = 2(2x) + 2(x) = 4x + 2x = 6x, and if x = 3 cm, then P = 6x = 18 cm.*

- Have students make, measure, and describe other polygons.

- Have students find polygons in abstract paintings, such as those by Piet Mondrian, and other art forms that use plane figures.

Center 2: Solid Figures

Materials: Show the Shapes reproducible, toothpicks, modeling clay, cardstock, protractors, metric rulers, compasses, scissors, rolling pins, plastic knives, water for moistening clay

Have students complete some or all of the following activity, depending on their ability levels. Display a copy of the **Show the Shapes reproducible (page 70)**, and provide a supply for students. Also display the following formulas: *Volume: cube, V = s3; prism, V = Bh; pyramid, V = 1/3Bh; cylinder, V = ᵖr2h. Remember: B stands for the area of the base (a polygon).*

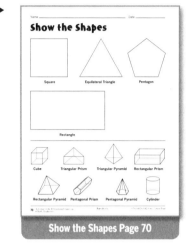

Show the Shapes Page 70

Give students the following instructions:

1. Look at the Show the Shapes reproducible to help you create toothpick models of these solid figures, using clay balls as vertices: cube, triangular prism, triangular pyramid, rectangular prism, rectangular pyramid, pentagonal prism, pentagonal pyramid.

2. Measure and describe the dimensions of each figure: length of each edge, perimeter of each face, area of each face, surface area of the entire figure, and volume of the figure.

3. Make another set of the same shapes, this time doubling the lengths. Predict changes in the measurements of perimeter, area, and volume. Then repeat Step 2.

4. Compare the two sets of shapes; write comparative equations.

5. Describe how these shapes might be used in architectural design.

Variation

Have students make solid clay models instead of toothpick models:

1. Glue the polygons from the top of the reproducible onto cardstock. Cut out the shapes to create templates for the faces of your figures, or create your own.

2. Roll out the clay to a thickness of 0.5 cm to 1.0 cm. Place templates on the clay, and use a plastic knife to cut around them to make faces.

3. Roll thin strands of clay. Place the strands along the edges of each face, connecting them together to form three-dimensional figures.

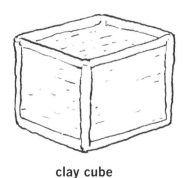

toothpick cube
with clay vertices

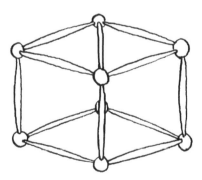

clay cube

Name _____ Date _____

Show the Shapes

Square

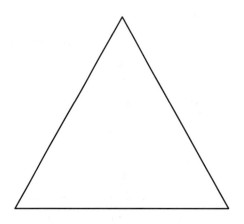

Equilateral Triangle

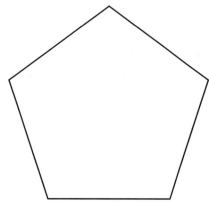

Pentagon

Rectangle

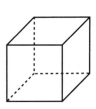

Cube

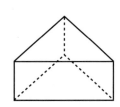

Triangular Prism

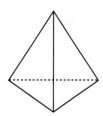

Triangular Pyramid

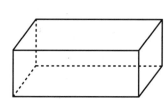

Rectangular Prism

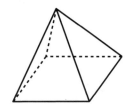

Rectangular Pyramid

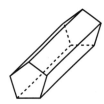

Pentagonal Prism

Pentagonal Pyramid

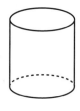

Cylinder

Reproducible   978-1-4129-5342-9 • © Corwin Press

CHAPTER 4

Measurement

Up to Scale

Standard
Measurement—Apply appropriate techniques, tools, and formulas to determine measurements.

Objective
Students will enlarge a picture to a given scale factor.

Materials
rulers, yardsticks, or T-squares
chart paper
crayons, markers, colored pencils

Strategy
Rehearsal

The National Council of Teachers of Mathematics (NCTM) recommends that middle-grade students solve problems involving construction or interpretation of scale drawings while working with ratio and proportionality. In this rehearsal activity, students enlarge a comic strip or CD cover by working with the panel's proportions.

1. Stimulate interest by having students bring in a color picture of their favorite cartoon or comic book character, comic strip, or CD cover. Photocopy pictures on which students can't draw.

2. Have students enlarge their pictures according to a given scale factor, such as 4:1 or 3:1. More advanced students may select a scale factor appropriate for the size of their picture and chart paper by measuring and using proportions.

3. Assign an appropriate unit of measure, such as inches or centimeters. (Allow advanced students to choose their own units of measure.) Tell students to not use a grid larger than $2'' \times 2''$ because it decreases the accuracy of the replication.

4. To enlarge the picture, have students draw a grid on the original picture and on the chart paper, using the scale factor and units of measure. (Start in the center and work outward. For example, if the ratio is 4:1 in centimeters, draw a one-centimeter grid on the original and a four-centimeter grid on the chart paper.)

5. Have students use pencil to copy the picture, square by square, from the small picture to the larger picture.

6. Instruct students to color the large drawing to match the original picture. Have them write the scale factor in the corner of the large drawing, and then attach the original picture to the top corner.

7. Display students' pictures around the classroom for all to enjoy!

Ideas for More Differentiation

Invite students with a high degree of mastery to also calculate the area of the original picture and the large drawing. Have them write the scale factor of the areas in the corner of the large drawing.

From Here to There

Standards

Measurement— Understand measurable attributes of objects and the
units, systems, and processes of measurement.
Apply appropriate techniques, tools, and formulas to determine
measurements.

Objective

Students will understand how ratios are used in a scale drawing to
estimate and calculate distances between cities.

Materials

Trip Planner reproducible
maps of the United States
rulers
markers
calculators
magnifying glasses (optional)

Strategies
Cooperative group
learning

Authentic task

   In this authentic task, students plan a cross-country trip, calculating
distances between cities using the map's scale. Distances may surprise
your students!

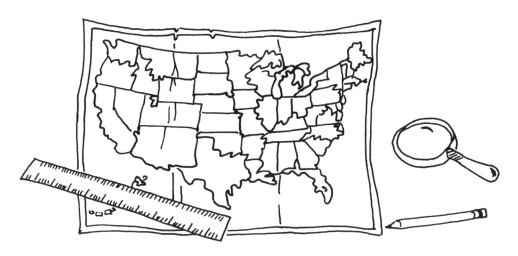

Trip Planner Page 75

1. Ask students if they have ever taken a road trip across the country.
   Invite them to share their experiences.

2. Divide the class into mixed-ability groups of three or four, and give
   each student a **Trip Planner reproducible (page 75)** and a map of the
   United States.

3. Tell students that they will plan a car trip across the country from Boston, Massachusetts, to San Francisco, California. They must stop at five different cities along the way and calculate the distance traveled for each part of the journey. Their goal is to find the shortest distance for their route. Assign the same five cities to the class, or allow students to choose their own.

4. Have students mark their route on a map and use the map's scale to determine the distance in both miles and kilometers. Remind them to use the conversion *1 mi = 1.6 km*. Suggest that they use pencil to mark possible routes from city to city, and then use a marker to retrace the shortest route.

5. Circulate around the room as students are working, providing assistance as needed. Ask guiding questions such as: *What route has the shortest distance between (city name) and (city name)? What geological features might make your trip more difficult? How might you find a more direct route to your destination?*

6. Check that students understand how to calculate travel time for each part of their trip using an average speed of 65 miles per hour. Ask: *Why might actual travel time differ from calculated travel time?* (delays due to traffic or weather) When calculating the total number of days, students can only include a maximum of ten hours of travel time per day. Discuss other factors that take up time, such as stopping for gas, food, and sleep.

7. After completing their Trip Planners, invite each group to share their results with the class. Encourage students to justify and give reasons why their route is the best.

Extend the Activity

- Suggest that students use online Internet Web sites such as MapQuest® at *www.mapquest.com* to help them determine routes, distances, and travel times from city to city.

- Display the price of gasoline in your area. Have students use that information to calculate the cost of driving if their car can travel 35 miles per gallon. Students might also research the current gas prices in each city and use those values to calculate costs.

- Invite students to include the cost of other expenses, such as food, lodging, and entertainment.

Trip Planner

Directions: Plan a car trip from Boston, MA, to San Francisco, CA. Use a map to determine the shortest route. You must stop at five cities along the way. Calculate the shortest distance for each leg of your trip.

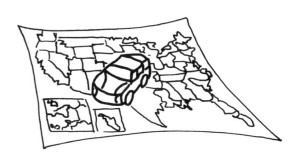

Starting City	Ending City	Inches on the Map	Miles (Kilometers)	Travel Time (at 65 mph)

Total distance: _____

Total time: _____

Total days (traveling ten hours per day max.): _____

What other factors should you consider when planning for this trip?
Make a list.

_____

_____

_____

_____

_____

Everyone Likes Pi!

Standards
Measurement—Apply appropriate techniques, tools, and formulas to determine measurements.
Understand measurable attributes of objects and the units, systems, and processes of measurement.

Objective
Students will use data about the circumference and diameter of circular objects to discover the value of pi. They will then use the formula to find the circumference of circles.

Materials
Paper Circles reproducible
Everyone Likes Pi! reproducibles
circular objects (plates, cups, bowls, cans)
metric tape measures (or string, scissors, and metric rulers)
calculators
dictionary

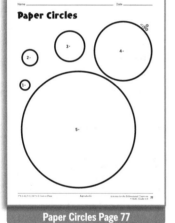

Paper Circles Page 77

This hands-on center activity helps students discover that the ratio of circumference to diameter is a constant that applies to all circles. They will gain a deeper understanding of the fundamental concept of pi. Students can work in center groups, in pairs, or individually.

Gather a collection of circular objects, including cutout circles from ◄ the **Paper Circles reproducible (Page 77)**. Put the objects in a center, along with a set of the **Everyone Likes Pi! reproducibles (pages 78–79)**. Invite students to measure five different objects. Then have them write the ratio of C/d (circumference to diameter) and divide with a calculator to convert the ratio to decimal form, rounding to the nearest thousandth.

Ideas for More Differentiation
- Have high-degree mastery students use a graphing calculator to graph diameter and circumference. Then use the linear regression to find the equation.

- Create a History of Pi Center where students can research mathematicians who calculated the value of pi or a timeline of the history of pi. Possible mathematicians could include the ancient Babylonians, the Rhind Papyrus, Archimedes of Syracuse, Ptolemy, Liu Hui, or Ludolph van Ceulen. Have students write a report or present their findings.

Paper Circles

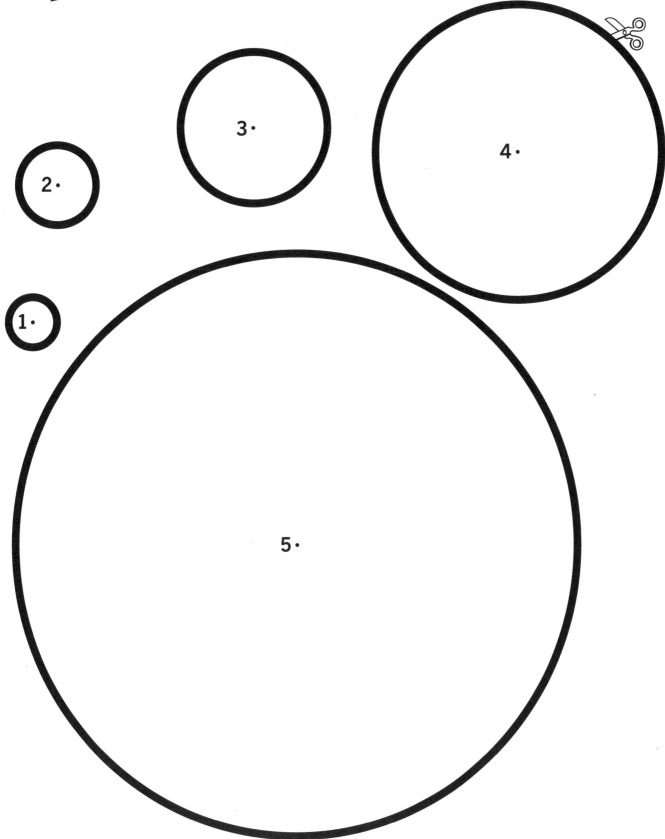

Name _____ Date _____

Everyone Likes Pi! Part 1

Directions: Measure the circumference and diameter of five different circular objects. Complete the chart, and answer the questions. Use a calculator to help you change the ratios to decimal form. Round your answers to the nearest thousandth.

Name of Object	Circumference (C)	Diameter (d)	Ratio (C/d) in Decimal Form
1.			
2.			
3.			
4.			
5.			

1. What do you notice about the relationship of circumference to diameter?

   _____

   _____

2. Mathematicians call this ratio *pi*. In your own words, define *pi*.

   _____

   _____

3. Look up the definition of *pi* in the dictionary. Write the definition and symbol.

   _____

   _____

4. How close do your ratios come to 3.14? Why might they be slightly different?

   _____

   _____

978-1-4129-5234-9 • © Corwin Press

Name _____ Date _____

Everyone Likes Pi! Part 2

Directions: Answer the questions. Use a calculator to help you.

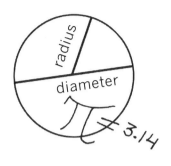

1. If you know the diameter of a circle, how can you find the circumference without measuring? Explain in words and then write an algebraic formula using C (circumference) and d (diameter).

_____

_____

2. Prove that your formula works. Use two diameter measurements from your chart in Part 1. Put them in your formula to calculate each circumference. Are your answers similar to the actual circumference measurements in your chart?

_____

3. If you know the radius of a circle, how can you find the circumference without measuring? Explain in words, and then write an algebraic formula using C (circumference) and r (radius).

_____

_____

4. Prove that your formula works. Measure the radius of two circles from your chart in Part 1. Put them in your formula to calculate each circumference. Are your answers similar to the actual circumference measurements in your chart?

_____

5. What other measurements and mathematical observations can you make about the circular objects, such as the paper circles? Write your ideas. Use formulas.

_____

_____

_____

Interior Decorator

Strategy

Authentic task

Standards

Measurement—Understand measurable attributes of objects and the units, systems, and processes of measurement.

Apply appropriate techniques, tools, and formulas to determine measurements.

Objective

Students use their knowledge of area and a floor plan to determine the amount of carpet to be purchased.

Materials

Floor Plan reproducible

tiles or slate pieces of various sizes

carpet advertisements

calculators (optional)

Invite students to participate in an authentic task to solve problems involving area and perimeter. In this real-world activity, students examine a floor plan to calculate the amount of tile and carpet needed to cover the floor areas.

1. Prior to the activity, label the tiles and slate with different prices. Then invite students to brainstorm careers in which people use measurement, such as carpenters, architects, interior decorators, and chefs.

2. Inform students they will be interior decorators for a day. They have been hired by Mr. Sanchez to redecorate his condominium.

3. Give students a copy of the **Floor Plan reproducible (page 82)**. Review how to read the floor plan.

4. Divide the class into mixed-ability groups of three or four. Give each group two tiles and/or slate and a carpet advertisement.

5. Explain that Mr. Sanchez wants to use tile or slate on his bathroom and kitchen floors, and he wants to put carpet on the remaining floor areas of his condo. Each group will present two types of carpet options and determine the flooring for the kitchen and bathroom. They will determine the amount needed for each, as well as the cost, and then make a presentation to the class.

Floor Plan Page 82

6. While students work in their groups, circulate around the room, assisting as needed. Help students figure out the most attractive and cost-effective options for Mr. Sanchez.

7. Then invite each group to present their design options to the class. Encourage students to explain the reasoning for thier flooring choices.

Ideas for More Differentiation

Have students with a high degree of mastery find an average cost for wallpaper and paint, as well. For this activity, ask them to assume that the condo walls are nine feet high.

Floor Plan

Directions: Mr. Sanchez wants new carpet in his family room and bedroom and new tile in his kitchen and bathroom. Calculate the area of each room. Determine the cost for both the carpet and the tile.

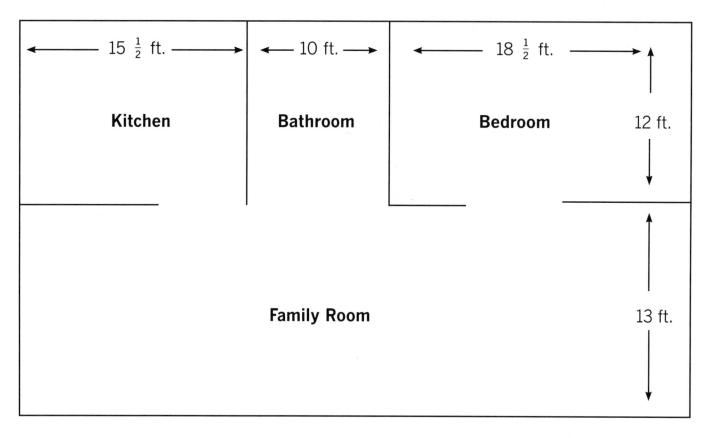

Kitchen: _____

_____

Bathroom: _____

_____

Family Room: _____

_____

Bedroom: _____

_____

Marvelous Measurements

Standard

Measurement—Understand measurable attributes of objects and the units, systems, and processes of measurement.

Strategies

Multiple intelligences

Adjustable project

Objective

Students will choose a project to show their knowledge of metric and customary units of measure.

Adjustable projects give students a choice of activities that appeal to a variety of learning styles and preferences. These flexible projects allow students to work at their own pace and readiness levels. In order to support all students, make a list of activities from which students can choose to "show what they know."

In middle school, students compare and convert units of measure for length, weight/mass, and volume within the customary system and metric systems. Provide students with the following choices to demonstrate their knowledge of measurement. They may work alone or with a partner.

- Use a computer to create a Microsoft® PowerPoint® presentation showing the relationships between metric and customary units of measure.

- Create a board game or card game converting units of measure.

- Keep track of the high and low temperatures in your area for one week. Use both Fahrenheit and Celsius scales. Make a chart and present it to the class. Be prepared to explain the difference between the scales.

- Write a persuasive letter to the President of the United States explaining why the nation should use the metric system.

- Create a poster showing customary and metric units of measure and how to convert from one to the other.

- Create a poem, song, or rap about the metric system and/or customary system.

- Convert a recipe to metric units of measure.

CHAPTER 5

Data Analysis and Probability

Car Wash Data

Standards
Data Analysis and Probability—Select and use appropriate statistical methods to analyze data.
Develop and evaluate inferences and predictions based on data.

Objective
Students will analyze data and create a graph appropriate for the given data set that best supports their recommended plan.

Materials
graph paper
tape or CD player
music tapes or CDs (classical, jazz)

Real-world tasks emphasize the importance of math in our daily lives. In this problem-solving activity, students analyze data involving real-life situations, which reinforces the relevance of data collection and other math calculations.

1. Present the following problem to students. Allow time for students to think about it by themselves. Invite volunteers to underline the key facts and goal.

    *Pinker Middle School needs to **raise $5,000** to purchase new computer software for their media center. The students decided to hold a **monthly car wash** to raise funds. The table shows results from their first car wash, in which they **charged $5 per car**. The committee is looking for recommendations to minimize the period of time needed to raise the funds and maximize profit. Devise a plan and use the data to support it.*

Data Table

	Saturday	Sunday
8:00 a.m. – 9:00 a.m.	26 cars	17 cars
9:00 a.m. – 10:00 a.m.	13 cars	9 cars
10:00 a.m. – 11:00 a.m.	22 cars	11 cars
11:00 a.m. – 12:00 p.m.	20 cars	25 cars

2. Review the data table with students. Prompt them to analyze and compare the number of cars washed each day and during each time period. For example, ask: *On which day were the most cars washed? During which time period were the most cars washed? The least cars washed? How much money was raised on Saturday? On Sunday? All together? How much more money is needed? What are some possible ways to raise the remaining money in less time? What are some possible promotional ideas or gimmicks you could use to attract customers?*

3. Pair up students with partners to share their ideas and formulate a better recommendation plan to the committee. Encourage partners to discuss other information they may need to make a better analysis, as well as assumptions they use in determining their plan (for example, knowing how many children are washing the cars or the location of the car wash). Each pair then creates a graph that is appropriate for the given data set and best supports their recommendations.

4. Have each group share their recommendations with the class. Invite the class to determine the validity and reasonability of each set of recommendations.

Ideas for More Differentiation

Stimulate your musical learners by playing Rose Royce's "Car Wash" while students formulate their plans and recommendations.

Mean, Median, Mode

Standards

Data Analysis and Probability—Select and use appropriate statistical methods to analyze data.
Develop and evaluate inferences and predictions based on data.

Objective

Students will select and use appropriate graphical representations and measures of central tendency for sets of data.

Middle-grade students need practice with measures of central tendency for data sets. Understanding how data values affect the mean and median is essential to data assessment.

1. Invite students to share what they know about the measures of central tendency: mean, median, and mode. Then write a list of test scores on the board, and work with students to organize the data, graph it, and find the mean, median, mode, and range.

2. Point out any outliers, and ask volunteers to determine how deleting them affects the measures of central tendency. Review different types of graphs—bar graph, line graph, line plot, stem-and-leaf plot, box-and-whisker plot. Check students' understanding, and refer to the following terms and definitions.

   Mean (Average): sum of the numbers divided by the number of addends
   Median: middle number in a set of data arranged from least to greatest; if there is an even number of data, it is the average of the middle two numbers
   Mode: number (or numbers) that occurs most often
   Range: spread of data; the difference between the greatest and least values
   Outliers: values that are much greater or much less than most of the data; *mean* is often affected by outliers, whereas *median* and *mode* usually are not
   Bar Graph: visual display comparing discrete data using bars
   Line Graph: display of connected points showing changes in data over time
   Line Plot: number line with Xs representing each number in a data set
   Stem-and-Leaf Plot: data display in which the numbers are shown as *stems* (tens digit) and *leaves* (ones digit) arranged in rows, from least to greatest

Box-and-Whisker Plot: data display in which the median is a central point dividing the data into two halves; the *lower quartile* (median of the data's lower half) and the *upper quartile* (median of the data's upper half) connect to form boxes; *whiskers* are drawn from the lower quartile to the lowest value and from the upper quartile to the greatest value.

Stem-and-Leaf Plot

Stem	Leaves
5	7 8 9
6	3 4 5 7
7	2 4

Key: 5|7 means 57

Box-and-Whisker Plot

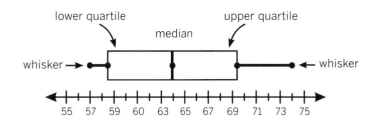

(data set: 57, 58, 59, 63, 64, 65, 67, 72, 74)

3. Invite students to choose one of the following projects or think of their own. Have them collect data; create at least one graph; analyze results, including mean, median, mode, and range; and write conclusions.
   - Conduct a survey about a current topic or event. Write a survey question that has at least five possible choices. Include at least 75 people in your survey.
   - Test your fitness daily for one week. Choose an activity that can be counted or timed, such as jumping rope, dribbling a basketball, pushups, weightlifting, or sprinting.
   - Compare prices of a chosen item, such as the price of a certain toy at different stores, the daily cost of food for your family, monthly phone bills, or college tuition.

4. Give students two weeks to collect data and complete the project. Then invite them to present their data and results to the class. Encourage classmates to ask questions and use calculators to check calculations. Have them assess each presentation using the following rubric (rank 1 to 4):
   - Sample set requirements were met.
   - Graph was appropriate and easy to ead.
   - Student accurately calculated mean, median, mode, and range.
   - Presentation was well organized and factual.

Graphing Rotation Reflection

Standard

Data Analysis and Probability—Select and use appropriate statistical methods to analyze data.

Objective

Students will reflect on reading and interpreting graphs.

Materials

chart paper
samples of various graphs
different dark-colored, broad-tipped markers
masking tape

In this activity, students work in cooperative groups, using the rotation-reflection strategy to review reading and interpreting graphs.

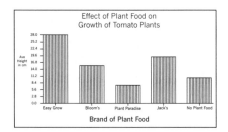

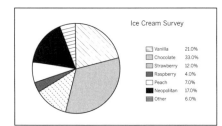

1. On sheets of chart paper, display graphs, such as histograms, line graphs, circle (pie) graphs, stem-and-leaf plots, line plots, box-and-whisker plots, and bar graphs. Post them around the classroom.

2. Divide the class into mixed-ability groups. Give each group a different-colored marker to keep track of what they write.

3. Decide on a set amount of time for each chart. Adjust time as needed; after several rotations, there may be not as much to write. Previous groups will have already written a lot. Give the signal for students to get started.

4. Have each group go to a chart and formulate questions and evaluate inferences and predictions based on the data. Have one student (the recorder) write the questions, inferences, and predictions on the chart.

5. After time is up, signal for groups to move to the next chart. Continue until all groups have visited each chart.

6. When the rotation is complete, each group remains at their last chart to answer each question and consolidate the inferences and predictions. Then review the questions, answers, inferences, and predictions with the whole class.

Probability Game

Standard
Data Analysis and Probability—Understand and apply basic concepts of probability.

Strategies
Focus activity

Game

Objective
Students will determine fractional probabilities in a game format.

Materials
Probability Game Sheet reproducible
decks of standard playing cards

A proper foundation of probability concepts is necessary in order to progress to higher-level concepts. By using a popular game format, students more easily understand and apply these basic concepts of probability.

1. Remind students that the probability of an event, i.e., the likelihood that it will occur, can be expressed as a fraction. Write on the board:

$$P(event) = \frac{number\ of\ outcomes\ in\ the\ event}{total\ number\ of\ possible\ outcomes}$$

2. Show students a standard deck of playing cards, and explain that they are going to calculate the probability of picking certain cards from the deck. Write the following list on the board, and invite students to help fill in the numbers:
   - *Total number of cards: 52*
   - *Number of each color (red or black): 26 red, 26 black*
   - *Number in each suit (hearts, diamonds, clubs, spades): 13 each*
   - *Number of sets of numeral cards and face cards: 13 sets*
   - *Number of each numeral or face card: 4 each*
   - *Number of red or black cards for each numeral or face card: 2 red, 2 black*
   - *Numeral and face cards in order: 2, 3, 4, 5, 6, 7, 8, 9, 10, J, Q, K, A*

3. Have students use the information on the board to determine the probability of choosing certain cards from the deck. For example: *What is the probability of choosing a red card? (26/52)*

18

21

Probability Game Sheet Page 91

A diamond? (13/52) A queen? (4/52) A red queen? (2/52) The numeral 6? (4/52) The 6 of clubs? (1/52) Any numeral less than 6? (16/52) Is there a greater probability of choosing a numeral card or a face card? (numeral; 36/52 > 16/52)

4. Choose a card from the deck, show students the card, and have them say the probability of choosing that card. Ask if the probability was likely or unlikely. Replace the card and repeat the process, asking students to pick cards.

5. Write the numerals and face card symbols in a row on the board, creating a 13-column tally chart. Pick eight cards from the deck, one card at a time. Ask volunteers to draw a tally mark on the board for each card picked. After picking a card, ask students a probability question about the remaining cards. For example, if the card is a 2: What is the probability of choosing another 2? (3/51) Is the probability greater than or less than choosing a king? (less) What is the probability of choosing a numeral less than 4? (7/51) Any card with a value less than 4? (11/51, including aces) Any card with a value greater than or equal to 4? (44/51, including aces) Explain that the probability changes after taking each card; it depends on the number of cards taken and the total number left.

6. Students then use what they learned to play the card game Twenty-One. Divide the class into groups of three or four. Give each group a deck of cards and each player a **Probability Game Sheet reproducible (page 91)**. Review how to play the game: Players are dealt cards, trying to get as close to the sum of 21 without going over and beat the dealer's total. Aces are worth 1 or 11. The dealer must take another card if he or she has 16 or less.

7. Invite students to play "face-up" Twenty-One, so all players can see the cards. Invite two volunteers to help you demonstrate the game, and model using the Probability Game Sheet. For example: Each player gets two cards (6 cards used, 46 cards left). You get a 9 and a 10, which is 19. You want a card less than or equal to 2. (P = 8/46) You decide the probability is not good, so you stay at 19. The dealer goes over 21, so you win. Mark tallies on your game sheet to show all the cards used: 9, 10, J, 6, 8, Q, 7, K, A.

8. Monitor students as they play the game, and offer assistance as needed. After groups complete all the rounds of their game, they can share and discuss results.

Name _____ Date _____

Probability Game Sheet

Directions: Use this sheet to help you play *Twenty-One*. For each round, write the probability of getting another "good" card after you get your initial pair. Draw tallies to show which cards have been used. Keep track of the cards, and use probability to help you decide how to play each round.

Round	Probability of a Good Card	Won or Lost?
1		
2		
3		
4		
5		
6		
7		
8		
9		
10		

Card Tally

2	3	4	5	6	7	8

9	10	J	Q	K	A

Puzzling Probability

Strategies

Cooperative group learning

Journaling

Standard

Data Analysis and Probability—Understand and apply basic concepts of probability.

Objective

Students will determine whether a game is fair or unfair through theoretical and experimental probability.

Materials

half-dozen egg cartons
dice
counters
marker

This hands-on activity allows students to use experimental and simple theoretical probability to understand the nature of sampling. Students will also make predictions from their investigations. This activity especially appeals to tactile/kinesthetic learners and mathematical/logical learners.

1. Divide the class into mixed-ability groups of three, and give each student an egg carton. Have one student in each group label the top sections of the carton *1, 2, 3* and the bottom sections *4, 5, 6*. Another student labels the top sections *8, 9, 10* and the bottom sections *12, 15, 16*. The last student labels the top sections *18, 20, 24* and the bottom sections *25, 30, 36*.

2. Inform each group that they will roll two dice, multiply the two numbers rolled, and place a counter in the egg carton section with that product. The student who fills his or her egg carton first wins.

3. Ask students: *Do you think this game is fair? Does everyone have an equal chance of winning? How can we determine whether the game is fair?* (experimental and theoretical probability)

4. Invite students to play the game, keeping a tally chart of the products rolled. As students are playing, circulate around the room, prompting them with questions such as: *What do you think of your results? Do they mean the game is fair? What would happen if you did the experiment again? Is there a way to improve the experiment?*

5. After students finish playing the game, initiate a class discussion.

Write each group's results on the board, and discuss them with the class.

6. Next, have students use theoretical probability to determine whether the game is fair. You may choose to assign certain groups the tree method or grid method. Or, depending on individual ability, allow students to discover the method. While students are working, prompt them with questions such as: *How many different outcomes are on the grid? What is the probability of rolling a score for the carton with 1, 2, 3, 4, 5, 6?*

The grid method is as follows:

x	1	2	3	4	5	6
1	1	2	3	4	5	6
2	2	4	6	8	10	12
3	3	6	9	12	15	18
4	4	8	12	16	20	24
5	5	10	15	20	25	30
6	6	12	18	24	30	36

The tree method is as follows:

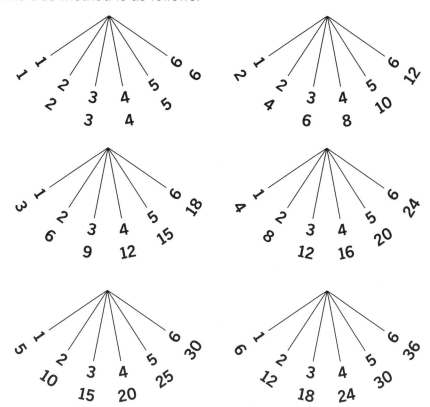

The probability of each carton is as follows (in sequence):

1, 2, 3, 4, 5, 6: $1/36 + 2/36 + 2/36 + 3/36 + 2/36 + 4/36 = 14/36$.

8, 9, 10, 12, 15, 16: $2/26 + 1/36 + 2/36 + 4/36 + 2/36 + 1/36 = 12/36$.

18, 20, 24, 25, 30, 36: $2/36 + 2/36 + 2/36 + 1/36 + 2/36 + 1/36 = 10/36$.

7. Invite students to share their theoretical probability results. Discuss whether the game is fair, who has the best chance of winning, and if there is a way to make the game fair.

8. Have students compare the experimental and theoretical results. Ask: *Are the results similar to each other?* Explain to students that the larger the sample pool in experimental probability, the closer the probability should be to theoretical probability (known as the Law of Large Numbers).

9. Have students reflect in their journals about what they learned.

References

Gregory, G. H., & Chapman, C. (2002). *Differentiated instructional strategies: One size doesn't fit all, second edition.* Thousand Oaks, CA: Corwin Press.

History of π. (2006). In *Wikipedia: The Free Encyclopedia*. Retrieved December 11, 2006, from http://en.wikipedia.org/wiki/History_of_pi.

History topic: A chronology of π. (n.d.) Retrieved November 28, 2006, from the University of St. Andrews, School of Mathematical and Computational Sciences Web site: http://www-groups.dcs.st-and.ac.uk/~history/PrintHT/Pi_chronology.html.

Mondrian, P. (2006). In *Encyclopædia Britannica*. Retrieved December 11, 2006, from http://www.britannica.com/eb/article-9053336.

National Council of Teachers of Mathematics. (2005). *Principles and standards for school mathematics*. Reston, VA: National Council of Teachers of Mathematics (NCTM).

National Council for the Social Studies. (2002). *Expectations of excellence: Curriculum standards for social studies*. Silver Spring, MD: National Council for the Social Studies (NCSS).

National Council of Teachers of English and International Reading Association. (1996). *Standards for the English language arts*. Urbana, IL: National Council of Teachers of English (NCTE).

National Research Council. (2005). *National science education standards*. Washington, DC: National Academy Press.

Answer Key

Interior Angles of Polygons (pages 46–47)

Quadrilateral
1. Any 4-sided closed figure with 1 diagonal drawn from a vertex.
2. 4 sides; 2 triangles
3. No. Students may use drawings to prove their answer.
4. 360°
5. Answers will vary.
6. No. The sum of the angles of any triangle is always 180°.

Pentagon
1. Any 5-sided closed figure with 2 diagonals drawn from a vertex.
2. 5 sides; 3 triangles
3. No. Students may use drawings to prove their answer.
4. 540°
5. Answers will vary.
6. No. The sum of the angles of any triangle is always 180°.

Hexagon
1. Any 6-sided closed figure with 3 diagonals drawn from a vertex.
2. 6 sides; 4 triangles
3. No. Students may use drawings to prove their answer.
4. 720°
5. Answers will vary.
6. No. The sum of the angles of any triangle is always 180°.

Heptagon
1. Any 7-sided closed figure with 4 diagonals drawn from a vertex.
2. 7 sides; 5 triangles
3. No. Students may use drawings to prove their answer.
4. 900°
5. Answers will vary.
6. No. The sum of the angles of any triangle is always 180°.

Octagon
1. Any 8-sided closed figure with 5 diagonals drawn from a vertex
2. 8 sides; 6 triangles
3. No. Students may use drawings to prove their answer.
4. 1,080°
5. Answers will vary.
6. No. The sum of the angles of any triangle is always 180°.

Nonagon
1. Any 9-sided closed figure with 6 diagonals drawn from a vertex
2. 9 sides; 7 triangles
3. No. Students may use drawings to prove their answer.
4. 1,260°
5. Answers will vary.
6. No. The sum of the angles of any triangle is always 180°.

Polygons Angles Table (page 48)

Triangle	3	1	180°
Quadrilateral	4	2	360°
Pentagon	5	3	540°
Hexagon	6	4	720°
Heptagon	7	5	900°
Octagon	8	6	1,080°
Nonagon	9	7	1,260°

1. For a polygon with n sides, $n - 2$ = number of triangles formed.
2. For every side added, the number of triangles formed also increases by one.
3. For every added side, another triangle can be formed, and the sum of the interior angles increases by 180°.
4. 16 triangles; 16 x 180° = 2,880°
5. $(n - 2)$ x 180°

Special Quadrilaterals (page 54)

	At least one pair of parallel sides	Opposite sides parallel	Opposite sides congruent	All sides congruent	Opposite angles congruent	All right angles
Parallelogram	✓	✓			✓	
Rectangle	✓	✓	✓		✓	✓
Rhombus	✓	✓	✓	✓	✓	
Square	✓	✓	✓	✓	✓	✓
Trapezoid	✓					

Quadrilateral Relationships (page 55)

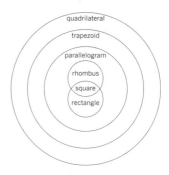

Angles/Transversals Guide (pages 65–66)

Vertical Angles: 4 pairs (1 & 4, 2 & 3, 5 & 8, 6 & 7); 2 pairs acute, 2 pairs obtuse; each pair is congruent; all acute are congruent; all obtuse are congruent.

Alternate Interior Angles: 2 pairs (3 & 6, 4 & 5); each pair congruent.

Alternate Exterior Angles: 2 pairs (1 & 8, 2 & 7); each pair congruent.

Corresponding Angles: 4 pairs (4 & 8, 2 & 6, 3 & 7, 1 & 5); each pair is congruent; all acute are congruent; all obtuse are congruent.

Consecutive Interior Angles: 2 pairs (4 & 6, 3 & 5); each pair supplementary (sum of 180°).

Consecutive Exterior Angles: 2 pairs (2 & 8, 1 & 7); each pair supplementary (sum of 180°).

Everyone Likes Pi! Part 1 (page 78)

1. All of the ratios are about 3.14.
2. Answers will vary.
3. Possible answer: pi is the ratio of the circumference of any circle to its diameter; approximately equal to 3.14 or 22/7; it is an endless decimal.
4. Possible answer: A difference in values may be due to 3.14 being only an approximate value for pi, and inaccuracies in measuring and calculations.

Everyone Likes Pi! Part 2 (page 79)

1. $C = d\pi$, so use the value of d times the value of π, or (d)(3.14).
2. Answers will vary.
3. $C = 2\pi r$, so use twice the value of r times the value of π, or 2(r)(3.14).
4–5. Answers will vary.